# Breathers of an Ampler Day

*Victorian Views of Heaven*

— IAN BRADLEY —

Sacristy Press

**Sacristy Press**
PO Box 612, Durham, DH1 9HT

www.sacristy.co.uk

First published in 2023 by Sacristy Press, Durham

Copyright © Ian Bradley 2023
The moral rights of the author have been asserted.

All rights reserved, no part of this publication may be reproduced or transmitted in any form or by any means, electronic, mechanical photocopying, documentary, film or in any other format without prior written permission of the publisher.

Every reasonable effort has been made to trace the copyright holders of material reproduced in this book, but if any have been inadvertently overlooked the publisher would be glad to hear from them.

Sacristy Limited, registered in England & Wales, number 7565667

**British Library Cataloguing-in-Publication Data**
A catalogue record for the book is available from the British Library

Paperback ISBN 978-1-78959-291-7
Hardback ISBN 978-1-78959-306-8

*Trust that those we call the dead*
*Are breathers of an ampler day*
*For ever nobler ends.*

*Alfred Tennyson,* In Memoriam

# Contents

**Preface** .................................................................. v
**Introduction** ........................................................... 1

Chapter 1. "There is a happy land, far, far away" .................. 19
Chapter 2. "How fares it with the happy dead?" ................... 34
Chapter 3. "I travel to meet a friend" ............................. 47
Chapter 4. "It's oh in Paradise that I fain would be" ................ 60
Chapter 5. "We know them living unto Thee" ..................... 78
Chapter 6. "Rest without ceasing to work" ........................ 90
Chapter 7. "I give Thee back the life I owe, that in Thine ocean's depths its flow may richer, fuller be" ........................ 105
Chapter 8. "A grand mysterious harmony floods me" .............. 123
Chapter 9. "The caterpillar dies into the butterfly" ................ 135
Chapter 10. "The heart still overrules the head" .................. 155

**Conclusion** .............................................................. 172

# Preface

Like all my books, of which this is the forty-sixth (I think!), this one is deeply personal and expressive of my own faith and enthusiasms. It is the third of a trilogy on death and the afterlife which has occupied me since I attained the age of three score years and ten in 2020. The first, *The Quiet Haven: An Anthology of Readings on Death and Heaven*, was published in 2021 by Darton, Longman & Todd. The second, *The Coffin Roads: Journeys to the West*, exploring Highland and Hebridean attitudes to dying, death, mourning, grieving and the afterlife, was published by Birlinn in 2022. This book completes the trilogy, and in many ways takes me full circle to a subject that has preoccupied me since my teenage years. The notebook that I still preserve of my school essays contains a personal meditation on heaven that I wrote at the age of 16. It includes a poem, which my English master described as Betjemanesque—I think this was intended as a compliment. Alongside copious references to trumpets and angelic choirs, it has the line "calm yet lively, full yet striving", expressing my conviction that there must be strenuous activity as well as rest in heaven. Little did I realize then that similar sentiments animated such eminent nineteenth-century theological minds as F. D. Maurice, Benjamin Jowett and W. E. Gladstone, who were later to become among my greatest heroes.

In late 1968, as a callow first-year undergraduate at New College, Oxford, I knocked on the door of the assistant chaplain's room in the front quad to unload on him my fears and doubts about the doctrine of eternal punishment, which troubled me considerably. I am not sure that he completely allayed them, but maybe our conversation helped him in some small way with the writing of his seminal study, *Hell and the Victorians*, which was published in 1974 and to which I have returned many times in the preparation of this work. Indeed, 50 years on from its publication, I offer my book on Victorian views of heaven as a posthumous tribute to Geoffrey Rowell, who went on to become chaplain of Keble College, Oxford, Bishop of Basingstoke (much to the delight of all his Gilbert and Sullivan-loving friends), and finally Bishop of Gibraltar in Europe before he died in 2017. When we met periodically in latter years, he used to remark that neither of us had changed our theological position one iota from that first meeting—he remained a staunch and very high Anglo-Catholic; I remained, in his words, "a classic and unreconstructed nineteenth-century liberal idealist", a sobriquet which I am quite happy to accept.

This book also comes out nearly 50 years after the publication of my own very first book, *The Call to Seriousness: The Evangelical Impact on the Victorians*, which derived from my 1974 Oxford doctoral thesis on "The Politics of Godliness: Evangelicals in Parliament, 1784–1832". I found much to commend in the theology and active practical Christianity of nineteenth-century Evangelicals. I have subsequently written sympathetically about Victorian Nonconformists, notably in *Enlightened Entrepreneurs* and in *The Optimists: Themes and Personalities in Victorian Liberalism*. More recently I have written much about the more mystical and Catholic traditions of Celtic Christianity and pilgrimage. But my greatest affection and admiration has throughout remained with the exponents of the gentle, eirenic, tentative, open and deeply pastoral theology of the Victorian Broad Church movement as represented in the writings of Alfred Tennyson, F. D. Maurice, George Matheson, John Ellerton and others who feature much in the pages that follow. They have been, and are still, my greatest mentors and soul friends, the ones with whom I feel most at home.

The other book to which I have had frequent recourse is Michael Wheeler's magisterial *Death and the Future Life in Victorian Literature and Theology*, first published in 1990. We cover some of the same ground, but there are enough differences, I hope, to justify my entering an area which he has written about so illuminatingly. He has no mentions, for example, of Ellerton, Matheson, Adelaide Procter or several others who figure prominently in my book. I have also gained from reading Robert Cecil's *The Masks of Death: Changing Attitudes in the Nineteenth Century* (1991), and thank the author's son, also Robert, for kindly sending me a copy.

This may be my last theological work, although I am not making any final predictions, and I am conscious of those, not least my contemporary liberal theological hero, Richard Holloway, who have written several "last testaments", and all the better that they have. The Victorians who appear in the chapters that follow have been my constant, faithful and treasured companions throughout my life and will, I trust, remain so in the next life. I hope that others, too, may find consolation and encouragement from them as we prepare for the final pilgrimage which awaits us all as we cast off, cross the bar and return to the ocean depths of God's love.

# Introduction

"How fares it with the happy dead?" The question that Alfred Tennyson, the nation's favourite poet, posed at the midway point in his widely read epic *In Memoriam*, itself published at the midway point in the nineteenth century, struck a deep chord with his contemporaries and compatriots. The Poet Laureate both represented and helped to shape the Victorians' view of the afterlife and their hope of heaven. His question mark is significant. Like Tennyson, many Victorians approached the subject with a degree of hesitancy and uncertainty, faintly trusting, as he did, the larger hope. But they shared his conviction that the lot of the dead is essentially a happy one and that, as "the breathers of an ampler day for ever nobler ends", they enjoy a better and happier life in heaven than the living do on earth.

The Victorians thought, wrote, preached and sang a great deal more about death and what might follow it than we do today. Novels were in no small measure judged by and appreciated for the power and pathos of their death bed scenes, with those involving Paul in *Dombey and Sons* and Little Nell in *The Old Curiosity Shop* generally reckoned to be among the best and most affecting. Ninety hymns in the 1889 edition of *Hymns Ancient & Modern* deal primarily with the experience of death and dying. By contrast, there is not a single hymn on the subject in its current successor, the 2013 *Ancient & Modern: Hymns and Songs for Refreshing Worship*. Nonconformist hymnals provided similar fare, as in the substantial section of the 1886 *Congregational Psalmist Hymnal* headed "Death and the Grave". Some of the most popular parlour ballads of the period feature heroic deaths, cold and cheerless tombs and deep-sea graves. They were sung to suitably hushed and sepulchral melodies, none more so than that provided by the life-loving Arthur Sullivan for Adelaide Procter's maudlin verses about meeting "Death's Dark Angel" and hearing the last Amen in heaven, which made "The Lost Chord" the best-selling song in Britain throughout the last quarter of the nineteenth century.

The tone of these literary and musical treatments of death was overwhelmingly positive. They reflected a widespread outlook among Victorian Christians that death was something to be looked forward to rather than dreaded. Frederick William Faber, the popular poet and priest who converted from Anglicanism to Roman Catholicism, spoke for many in his enthusiastic evocation of its joyful and liberating character:

> O grave and pleasant cheer of death! How it softens our hearts and without pain kills the spirit of the world within our hearts! It draws us towards God, filling us with strength and banishing our fears, and sanctifying us by the pathos of its sweetness. When we are weary and hemmed in by life, close and hot and crowded, when we are in strife and self-dissatisfied, we have only to look out in our imagination over wood and hill, and sunny earth and starlit mountains, and the broad seas whose blue waters are jewelled with bright islands, and rest ourselves on the sweet thought of the diligent, ubiquitous benignity of death.[1]

It is not surprising that historians often refer to "the Victorian celebration of death".[2] Its wider cultural manifestations included ostentatious funerals and mourning rituals with extensive use of floral tributes, black crêpe, jet jewellery, black-edged writing paper, cards and envelopes, tears embroidered on handkerchiefs, and the wearing of mourning dress for months and sometimes several years. The Victorian age saw the rise of the funeral industry and the emergence of a new profession, undertakers, who took over many of the functions previously performed by the clergy. In a similar and parallel way, death moved beyond the confines of the church as cemeteries took over from overcrowded church graveyards. The first cemetery in London opened in Kensal Green in 1832—the same year that the Glasgow Necropolis opened—and between 1850 and 1900, 66 cemeteries were established in the capital, filled with elaborate monuments more often than not surmounted by weeping angels.

At one level, this focus on what might be called the accoutrements of death was a result of increasing wealth and the rise of an affluent middle class. For the historian David Cannadine, "The Victorian celebration of death was not so much a golden age of effective psychological support as a bonanza of commercial exploitation." The ostentatious funerals, extensive rituals and paraphernalia of mourning were "more an assertion of status than a means of assuaging sorrow, a display of conspicuous consumption rather than an exercise in grief therapy, from which the chief beneficiary was more likely to be the undertaker than the widow".[3] This is also the view of the French historian Philippe Ariès, who wrote several books about changes in western attitudes towards death over the last thousand or more years. He relates the growing interest in death in the nineteenth century largely to socio-economic factors, with rising wealth enabling the development of elaborate funerals, grand cemeteries and a whole industry of mourning.[4]

I do not myself agree with this analysis. The prime reason why the Victorians focused so much more on death than we do today is surely because it was an ever-present reality, directly touching more people much more closely and much more often than it does now. Nowadays, it is quite common for people to have little if any direct experience of death until late adulthood. One hundred and fifty years ago, there were few young adults who had not experienced the loss of a close contemporary, and many children had witnessed the death of a sibling. Death mostly happened at home rather than out of sight in a curtained-off hospital bed or care home. It was more public, more physical, and altogether more present.

The statistics behind the Victorian experience of death are stark. The average life expectancy of someone born in Britain in 1837, the year of Victoria's accession, was just 39 years, less than half the current figure of 81. In London, the average age of death for tradesmen and clerks was 25 and for labourers just 22. Infant mortality (death within the first year of life) stood at 150 per 1000 births and actually rose through the century, reaching 160 per 1000 births in 1899—the current level is just over three per 1000. In Manchester in 1840, 57 per cent of working-class children died before reaching the age of five, and the 1851 census revealed that 55 per cent of the population of Liverpool died before the age of 20. Infectious diseases, notably smallpox, consumption (tuberculosis), cholera, scarlet fever, measles, typhus, diphtheria and whooping cough were the main causes of death both in children and adults.

It was not just the working classes and those dwelling in the squalid, overcrowded slums of large industrial cities who suffered high levels of infant mortality. In the spring of 1856, while living in the airy and spacious deanery in the genteel precincts of Carlisle Cathedral close, Archibald Tait, later to become Archbishop of Canterbury, and his wife Catharine lost five daughters aged between one and ten years to scarlet fever in the space of five weeks. The almost unbearably moving journal that Catharine wrote about this experience illustrates how the death of children prompted thoughts of the next life and, in the case of strong Christian believers like her, an absolute certainty that the dead were destined for heaven, where they would in time be reunited with their family and friends. Gathering together her surviving children after the first death, of Charlotte (Chatty), who was just five, Catharine tells them that "the Good Shepherd had come for her and taken her into His arms to heaven".[5] Sitting later beside Chatty's open coffin, she reflects that "we know that we shall see her again, though not in this world".[6] Despite her own enormous sorrow, she finds herself asking as she sits by the bedside of the third child to die, Frances, aged four, "If her home in Heaven is ready, should I wish to keep her here?", and after the last death, of Mary (May) at the age of eight, she records simply "she has gone home".[7]

The reaction of Catharine Tait to her daughters' deaths, to which I will return a number of times in the pages that follow, underlines what will be one of the major themes of this book: that the Victorian view and vision of heaven was developed out of a desire for consolation and comfort in the face of intense grief, driven above all by pastoral considerations, with the heart ruling the head, and characterized by trusting, whether faintly as in the case of Tennyson and many others, or much more surely as for Catharine, "the larger hope".

It is the constant, inescapable encounter with it—not least in respect of children—that explains the Victorian preoccupation with death. This also produced a certain familiarity which resulted in there being much less fear of death than there is today. The Victorians did not share our modern obsession with keeping people alive at all costs, regardless of the quality of that extra life. Nineteenth-century doctors, patients and their families generally agreed that the terminal phase of an illness should not be prolonged by drugs or other medical intervention. They used the word "euthanasia" approvingly to signify a calm and easy death without the negative connotations that it has today. The overriding view in the medical profession, across the churches and in society at large, was that dying was a natural process which should be allowed to take its course and not prolonged or resisted with the kinds of intervention which are widely practised today.[8]

Not surprisingly, the prevalence of death and the consequent focus on it in the nineteenth century led to much more interest than there is now in what might follow it. We have already seen this in the case of Catharine Tait. One aspect of this was a huge rise of interest in spiritualism. The origin of modern spiritualism in the United Kingdom is often taken to be a visit made to London in 1852 by an American medium, Maria Hayden, who offered séances in fashionable salons. Interest in spiritualism took off spectacularly in the second half of the century. Gladstone, Thackeray and Dickens were among the many eminent Victorians who visited séances. Spiritualism provided an alternative theology, where death was seen as a seamless movement of transition, a passing over or passing on. There was no interruption or long period of slumbering in the grave, as suggested by orthodox Christian doctrine. Spirits moved straight to a new life or spirit land where they met departed loved ones.

Spiritualists had their own distinctive and somewhat eccentric take on what followed death, as illustrated by the letter that Sir Charles Isham, a Northamptonshire landowner and gardener credited with beginning the tradition of garden gnomes in the United Kingdom and a keen spiritualist, claimed that he had received from a dead friend:

> I am now residing in Jupiter, and am very happy, though thoroughly under the influence of 'King Saul' ... he is teaching me to fly gracefully ... I have a flower undergoing the process of materialisation for you, and will enclose it in this letter if it is solid enough to make the journey through the post.[9]

Although officially condemned by the Church, a good number of Victorian clergy found spiritualism very appealing. Feeling that it might rekindle the Christian faith, and particularly enhance belief in life after death, they criticized the Church for its negative attitude.

Spiritualism flourished partly because there was a considerable vacuum and a good deal of uncertainty in what the churches taught and thought about what followed death—as, indeed, there is even more today. It is a distinctly fuzzy and hazy area which is surprisingly little covered in the Bible, and when it is, it is with a certain amount of ambiguity. The fundamental distinction and tension between the Hellenistic Jewish emphasis on the immortality of the soul and the Pharisaic belief in bodily resurrection carried over into Christianity and was never fully resolved. Statements attributed to Jesus in the synoptic Gospels suggest that he perhaps inclined more to the latter, and believed in a relatively quick ascent of those who had died to heaven; John's Gospel seems to favour the Greek conception of immortality over the notion of resurrection; Paul in 1 Corinthians 15 writes in somewhat impenetrable language about new spiritual bodies; and the Book of Revelation presents a dramatic apocalyptic picture of a new heaven and new earth. As Geoffrey Rowell concludes, "It would be wrong to suppose that a coherent eschatology could be derived from the New Testament."[10] Much was left to the imagination, which is why poets have such a prominent role in putting forward a vision of heaven. Lucy Sharpe, a writer who came of Unitarian stock, was typical in her observation that "the form and manner of our last change is one of the subjects that our Heavenly Father has left undefined, that each child should adopt that view most consoling to his spirit".[11]

Lucy Sharpe's position that, given the uncertainty about what happened after death, the best thing was to adopt the view that one found most consoling was shared by many of her contemporaries. This led an increasing number of them to opt for the Platonic idea of the immortality of the soul rather than the Christian doctrine of bodily resurrection, particularly as it had traditionally been taught in terms of a literal rising from the graves on the last day. More orthodox Christians sought not to depart too far from St Paul's teaching, as shown by Catharine Tait's conviction that her children would sleep "till [God] clothes their mortal bodies with the full beauty of immortality".[12] But even they tended to eschew the word "resurrection" despite the clear statement in the Book of Common Prayer and in the burial services of nearly all other churches committing the dead "in sure and certain hope of the resurrection to eternal life". As will be explored in Chapter 10, several Victorian poets and preachers made interesting attempts to relate the Christian idea of resurrection to the cycle of decay and regeneration in the natural world and used the analogy of the butterfly emerging from the chrysalis to describe what happens to humans after death. But belief in a day of resurrection when bodies would literally rise from their graves steadily diminished. One reason for this was the gross overcrowding of burial plots and churchyards, which led to bodies being heaped on top of each other and bones misplaced. The coming of cremation in the later decades of Victoria's reign further weakened belief in a literal resurrection. The first cremation in Britain is thought to have taken place in Dorset in 1882 when the bodies of Lady Hanham and her daughter-in-law were cremated in a small, specially constructed furnace in an orchard. The first crematorium was established in Woking in 1885.[13]

The idea of immortality fitted with the increasingly individualistic approach of Victorian thought, in which the preservation of individual personality after death was seen as important. It also fitted with the idea of progress which was one of the most characteristic doctrines of the age. The strong emphasis on consolation, as evident in the writings of both Catharine Tait and Lucy Sharpe, and the growing liberalism in religious and philosophical thought further contributed to weakening traditional Christian teaching about the separation of the sheep and the goats with the latter being consigned to hell, and promoting instead a kind of benevolent universalism that conceived of most, if not all, people going to heaven. This approach stood in a tradition established by the third-century Egyptian theologian Origen and could claim biblical warrant in such texts as Acts 3:21 and Ephesians 1:10.

Although the overall mood was gradually shifting in favour of a consolatory universalism, there was still a strong continuing adherence within the churches to the doctrine of eternal punishment for the wicked, a category often taken to embrace the majority of the population, in the aftermath of a final and terrible Day of Judgment. This had, of course, been orthodox Christian doctrine for most of the history of the Church, particularly in the Middle Ages when so many churches were decorated with graphic frescoes showing the rising of the dead from their graves, either to descend into the eternal fires and sulphurous pits of hell or rise to the heavenly clouds.

Geoffrey Rowell rightly reflects that "there can be no doubt that the doctrine of everlasting punishment was a major concern for Christians for the greater part of the nineteenth century".[14] The extent to which it led intelligent people to give up on the Christian faith altogether is well illustrated in the figure of Lewis Farnell, a classical scholar who became Vice Chancellor of Oxford University in the 1920s. Farnell is particularly interesting in illustrating the huge impact that the deaths of close family members could have on the faith of Victorian intellectuals, both positively and negatively. In 1870, when he was 14, he suffered the loss of his beloved eldest brother, who died of a mild attack of scarlet fever, having just gained a double first at Oxford:

> I was told and I believed that I should see him again in heaven if I prepared myself so as to be worthy of that privilege. I therefore set my mind earnestly to this end, while I kept my resolve very carefully to myself; for I had more than the usual boy's reticence about my soul-experiences.

This triggered a period of intense religious fervour which led young Lewis into long periods of praying every day.

Four years later, when Lewis himself had just gone up to Oxford, his father died after a short illness that was probably undiagnosed appendicitis:

> The shock had one curious spiritual effect on me: it delivered me finally from part of the traditional dogmatism, the belief in hell or punishment after death, which has so rarely controlled the evil and has so often tormented the good. For I imagined that my father was not wholly 'orthodox'; and if orthodoxy proclaimed that happiness hereafter depended on the acceptance of its full creed, I would have none of it; for I was deeply convinced that he if anyone deserved that happiness, and I would have nothing to do with any dogma that threw doubt on his attaining it. But I then

found that to reject hell was to reject part of the New Testament. Therefore, as my brother's death first quickened religion in me, my father's quickened the earliest freedom of thought.[15]

It was not only for sensitive intellectuals like Farnell that hell was a major stumbling block to belief, although they were the ones who chiefly wrote about it and wrestled most conspicuously with their unease and doubts. Among the many letters received by the Anglican clergyman Frederic Farrar following the publication in 1878 of his book *Eternal Hope*, a key text in turning popular attention from hell to heaven (see pp. 93–4), was this one from a London vicar:

> There is no one thing which oppresses the minds of thoughtful men at the present day more than the popular idea that Christianity is committed to the affirmation of the everlasting damnation of the overwhelming majority of mankind. Among the lower class of unbelievers there is no greater stumbling block in the way of their acceptance of Christianity; and I know of no thoughtful man on whose mind the idea is not acting with great might. It is one of the most fruitful sources of modern unbelief.[16]

A clergyman who had worked for six years among the London poor told Farrar that the popular doctrine of hell excited the scorn of working men, and a Manchester curate expressed his opinion that many working men would become atheists if hellfire preaching continued.

The decline of belief in the doctrine of everlasting punishment is one of the most marked features of the changing climate of thought in the latter half of the nineteenth century. It is well chronicled in Geoffrey Rowell's book *Hell and the Victorians*. Among the main reasons for it was moral revulsion at the idea that a basically benevolent and good God could consign people who had not led particularly bad lives to eternal torment. This, as we have seen, was what troubled Lewis Farnell, and it was stated most famously by John Stuart Mill when he said, "I will call no being good who is not what I mean when I apply that epithet to my fellow creatures; and if such a creature can sentence me to hell for not so calling him, to hell I will go."[17] The new German school of biblical criticism, with its insistence that the Bible should be treated primarily as a historical text and not as the literal word of God, also had an impact as it was taken up in British universities and theological colleges from the 1850s onwards. As Geoffrey Rowell says, "There is a clear connection between belief in an infallible Bible and belief in Hell."[18] Increasing missionary endeavour and contact with those of other faiths, or of no faith, made many Christians uneasy with the idea that a large proportion of the human race was condemned to everlasting punishment simply because of never having encountered the Christian Gospel. In 1855, Bishop John Colenso of Natal, a leading liberal Broad Churchman who was one of the first Anglicans to apply biblical criticism and question the literal truth and historical accuracy of large parts of the Old Testament, asked how a Christian "could comfortably eat butter with his bread, ride in a carriage, wear a fine nap upon his coat, or enjoy one of the commonest blessings of daily life if he believed heathen souls to be perishing in their millions". To teach "the state of everlasting torment after death, of all impenitent sinners and unbelievers, including the whole of the heathen world" was, for him, to make incredible "the cardinal doctrine of the Gospel, the Fatherly relation to us of the Faithful creator".[19]

It took a considerable time for the idea of hell to be banished and a good many Evangelical, Anglo-Catholic and Roman Catholic clergy continued to preach hellfire sermons. Much of the credit for turning the tide, in the established Church at least, must go to F. D. Maurice, who is the subject of Chapter 6, and to his disciples, notably Frederic Farrar. Those Evangelicals who did drop the doctrine of everlasting punishment tended to opt instead for conditional immortality, also known as annihilationism, the idea that the wicked are simply annihilated rather than condemned to face eternal torment. Anglo-Catholics and Roman Catholics enthusiastically espoused the medieval doctrine of Purgatory, positing an intermediate state of cleansing and purification between death and judgment which was sometimes called Paradise. Geoffrey Rowell points out that the phrase "intermediate state" was, indeed, "characteristic of the nineteenth century".[20]

As fear of hell subsided, so hope of heaven came to occupy a much more prominent place in Victorian thought and imagination both at a popular level and among intellectuals. The growing interest and focus on heaven can be clearly discerned in the language of hymns. Heaven receives over 100 explicit mentions in the seminal 1889 edition of *Hymns Ancient & Modern*, and there are a further 43 references to Paradise and numerous other mentions of eternal life. Hell is mentioned in just 15 of the 638 hymns in that book, and only in four of those is it conceived of primarily as a place of pain and punishment. When the Australian historian Pat Jalland searched through the manuscript archives of 55 upper- and middle-class Victorian families for her book on *Death in the Victorian Family*, she found only two mentions of hell—one from the lapsed Catholic Wilfrid Scawen Blunt and the other from the freethinker Ada Lovelace. The overwhelming focus was rather "on the prospect of immortality in heaven".[21]

The Romantic movement undoubtedly played a part in switching the attention of poets, artists and theologians from hell to heaven. While the medieval imagination had dwelt on the graphic and ghastly torments of everlasting punishment, a preoccupation not ended by the Reformation, and the eighteenth-century Evangelical Revival had further stoked the flames of hellfire preaching, the romantic imagination of Samuel Taylor Coleridge and his nineteenth-century successors inspired a gentle liberal-minded idealism (precisely that mindset that Geoffrey Rowell rightly identified me as espousing). In his book *The Hour of Our Death*, Philippe Ariès suggested that Romanticism transformed death from something to be feared to something beautiful and emphasized the joys of heaven. Pointing out that the function of hell was moral whereas the function of heaven was consoling, he further argued that the shift of emphasis from the former to the latter in the nineteenth century also resulted from the growth of a new type of family relationship, which he called affectivity, which made family bonds much stronger and more eternal. It is certainly true, as we shall see, that the Victorians set considerable store by the promise and hope of being reunited with family members in heaven.

This romantic attachment to "the beautiful death" made heaven an essentially happy place, as suggested by Tennyson in the question he posed in *In Memoriam* One of the first books by a leading churchman to emphasize this theme, *The Happiness of the Blessed Considered as to the Particulars of their State*, by Richard Mant, Bishop of Down and Connor, was published in 1833, just four years before Victoria came to the throne, and went through numerous editions in the first three decades of her reign. It spawned a host of successors. In the 40 years following its publication, more than 40 popular books appeared with similar titles all portraying heaven as a home where friends and family would be reunited.

For some, predominantly Evangelicals, Anglo-Catholics and Roman Catholics, the happiness of heaven was to be found primarily in the opportunity which it offered of the continuous worship of God. In their imaginings of the heavenly state, angelic choirs equipped with harps and trumpets surrounding God's throne loomed large. But increasingly this traditional theocentric view was replaced by a much more anthropocentric notion of heaven where the emphasis was on sociability, community and personal interaction and development. Heaven was conceived less as a church and place of worship and more as a community and place of self-development. In their book *Heaven: A History*, Bernhard Lang and Colleen McDannell suggest that around the middle of the nineteenth century the traditional, static, theocentric view of heaven gave way to a much more dynamic concept, with service and education replacing worship as its primary activity. In another book, *Meeting in Heaven*, Lang echoes Ariès in noting an increasing focus in this period on the family rather than God or the Church. The expectation comes to be that heaven involves love, work and social and intellectual interaction and as such is an environment resembling that in which we live here and now. Overall, Lang finds nineteenth-century literature on heaven reflecting "a vague yet popular consensus" encompassing assurance of salvation and agreement that after death the soul goes immediately to heaven in order to enjoy eternal bliss. Notions of judgment and general resurrection are largely absent, and mention of hell pretty well disappears.[22]

The conviction that friends and family would be reunited, so strongly and movingly evidenced in Catharine Tait's reaction to her five daughters' deaths, was perhaps the key element in this new understanding of heaven as a happy home. This was not a new belief. Bernhard Lang and Colleen McDannell find its earliest expression in the writings of Bishop Cyprian of Carthage in the mid-third century. Despite the lack of any clear biblical warrant for this belief, it was held by several prominent eighteenth-century Evangelicals, including William Wilberforce and the hymnwriter James Montgomery, one of whose hymns contains the line

"There is a world above where parting is unknown".[23] It became much more widespread in the nineteenth century, becoming one of the most commonly held views as to what heaven would be like. The idea that friends and family would be reunited in heaven had been strongly canvassed in Richard Mant's *The Happiness of the Blessed*, which had as its subtitle *Their Recognition of Each Other in That State*. It was put forward even more emphatically in three books written in the early 1860s by William Branks, Church of Scotland minister of Torphichen in West Lothian, entitled *Heaven our Home*, *Life in Heaven* and *Meet for Heaven*, which became bestsellers. Branks presented heaven as having a clear location and emphasized the theme of friends and family being reunited there. The first chapter of *Heaven our Home*, entitled "Heaven A Locality", describes "an *etherialised, luminous, material habitation* in which the children of God are throughout eternity to dwell".[24] In the book's preface, Branks declares his determination to counter the negative views of heaven given by so many divines, "so utterly unsocial in their aspect", and calculated to repel the longings and aspirations of Christians rather than "allure their thoughts upwards". By contrast, his aim is to promote the idea of a "social heaven". For him, "A heaven from which *saint-friendship* and *social intercourse* among those who are in glory are excluded *is* not and *cannot* be a suitable abode for us, who have received from God's own plastic hand those *social affections* which we are to possess forever".[25]

One of those influenced by William Branks' comforting portrayal of heaven was Queen Victoria, who read *Heaven our Home* with Prince Albert in the last months of his life. It reinforced her already strong belief in an afterlife and her conviction that friends and family would be reunited after death. Victoria herself played a significant personal role in shaping the celebration of death with which her reign is associated, taking it to new heights by instituting what was effectively a new religious tradition: the holding of an annual memorial service for family members on the anniversary of their deaths. This began with Albert, who was commemorated after his death in December 1861 by an annual memorial service in Frogmore, where she constructed an immense mausoleum with the words "Farewell, best beloved, here at last I shall rest with thee, with thee in Christ I shall rise" inscribed above the entrance doors.

Victoria's lengthy period of mourning for Albert, when she wrapped herself in widow's weeds and withdrew from public life for over ten years, caused consternation to her ministers. Courtiers were similarly dismayed by what they regarded as the morbid and excessive grief and mourning which followed in the wake of all subsequent royal deaths. Yet in many ways the "crêpe pall" which so often descended on the court chimed in with popular sentiment and brought the Queen closer to the hearts of her subjects. In his recent spiritual biography of her, Michael Ledger-Lomas points to Victoria's obsessive absorption with the deaths not just of those in her extended family but also of members of the armed forces and tenants on the royal estates. Commenting on what he calls her "promiscuous grief" and noting how her conspicuous mourning rituals "used music and flowers to cast death as a gentle transition to another world continuous with this one", he writes that "they reflect how sentiment was coming to replace eschatology in thinking about the dead, and as such fastened the public's attention on Victoria as the nation's mourner-in-chief".[26]

Victoria frequently expressed her own belief in heaven and her certainty that it would be a place of reunion with loved ones in her visits to those living on the royal estates. On one such visit to a cottage in Windsor Great Park, she took the wasted hand of a woman who had been ill, saying, "I come not as a Queen, but as a Christian lady", and telling her, "Put your trust in Jesus, and you will soon be in a land where there is no pain. You are a widow, so am I; we shall soon meet our beloved ones." On another occasion, when asked by the Queen what she could do for her, a "lonely cottager" said she would be very glad "if Your Majesty would just promise to meet me in Heaven". Softly and firmly came the Queen's reply: "I shall do so in virtue of the blood of the Lord Jesus Christ."[27]

The Queen's view of heaven was confirmed and doubtless in no small part further shaped by the sermons of those clergy who were closest to her. Preaching in the dining room of Balmoral in the May following Albert's death, her favourite chaplain, the Church of Scotland minister Norman Macleod, spoke extempore of "the blessedness of suffering in bringing us nearer to our eternal home, where we should all be together, and where our dear ones were gone on before us".[28] Another much favoured Scottish Presbyterian minister, John Caird, preached before her in similar terms, evoking "the nearness of sympathetic loving souls, which no distance could divide" and softening the "agony of losing those we love" with the reflection that they had "great work to do elsewhere".[29] Preaching in Prince Albert's old room at Windsor Castle on the first anniversary of his death on 14 December 1862, Arthur Stanley, the newly appointed Dean of Westminster, declared his belief that the dead had merely taken the first of "many steps, in that upward, onward ascent, by which the blessed spirit of the departed rises ever higher and higher into communion with the Fountain of all Wisdom and Goodness". He bracketed Albert's death and that of Christ as similar "great visitations ... wide rents in the veil between this world and the next", which alerted the living to the prospect of "a nearer union with God".[30]

Similar sentiments were expressed by the clergy in the aftermath of subsequent royal deaths. Preaching before the Prince of Wales (later Edward VII) and his wife Princess Alexandra of Denmark following the death through influenza of their eldest son, Albert Victor, Duke of Clarence, on the eve of his marriage in January 1892, James Fleming, vicar of St Michael's, Chester Square, and chaplain in ordinary to the Queen, posed the "intense" question, "Shall we know each other in another world?" He answered it with a thunderous "Yes", assuring the mourning parents that "their separation from their gentle Prince-boy is but temporary, their re-union with him shall be eternal before the throne of God".[31] The Duke's funeral service at St George's, Windsor, ended at Princess Alexandra's request with the anthem "Brother, thou art Gone Before Us", written by Henry Hart Milman before he became Dean of St Paul's Cathedral and set by Arthur Sullivan. This immensely popular funeral anthem addressed the departed with the assurance that "thy saintly soul is flown, / where tears are wiped from every eye, and sorrows are unknown", and went on to promise "thou art sure to meet the good, whom on earth thou lovedst best". Michael Ledger-Lomas comments that "its message that the next world was a continuation of this one made it a favourite at funerals in the royal household".[32]

This book explores the views of heaven which were held and propagated by some of Victoria's best known and most influential subjects, and by others less illustrious. In many respects, they echo the Queen's own strong convictions. It moves from popular hymns and

Sunday school songs through the verses of three popular poets, Alfred Tennyson, Christina Rossetti and Adelaide Proctor, to the writings and sermons of four leading churchmen and theologians, the Anglicans John Ellerton and F. D. Maurice, the Presbyterian George Matheson and the Roman Catholic John Henry Newman. There are also chapters exploring the views of those such as Charles Kingsley, Frederick Robertson, John Clare and Ellice Hopkins who drew analogies from the cycle of death and rebirth in the natural world, and of poets and philosophers who were rather more on the fringes of faith, such as Francis Newman, William Henry Clough, William Greg and Henry Sidgwick. In addition to these famous names, the thoughts and ideas of many lesser-known figures are also considered.

What follows is by no means an exhaustive survey of Victorian views of the afterlife. I have chosen what I hope is a representative set of voices, although there is a preponderance of those from the Broad Church liberal tradition. This is a reflection not just of my own prejudices but also of what became the dominant outlook at both a popular and academic level, expressed in an emphasis on consolation and pastoral concern, a tendency to let the heart rule the head, and to trust, however faintly and tentatively, in the larger hope and embrace something close to universalism. As we have already noted, there was widespread agreement that heaven was essentially a happy and a homely place where loved ones would be reunited and life would carry on in many ways as it had on earth. There were widely different views of what it would be like, with some emphasizing rest and worship and viewing it as an eternal Sabbath, and others rather envisaging it as a place of strenuous activity, progressive development and self-improvement. The "intermediate state" of sleep, Paradise or Purgatory was made much of by some, largely ignored by others and understood by those who did acknowledge it in various different ways.

Ultimately all thought about heaven is very largely an exercise in imaginative speculation founded on the hints that are given in scripture. What is striking about those whose views on the subject are quoted and analysed in this volume is not only the richness of their imaginations and the elegance of their writing, but also the conviction that they nearly all share that there must be a heaven, and that they, and we, are bound for that happy land.

# Notes

1. Frederick William Faber, *Notes on Doctrinal and Spiritual Subjects*, Vol. II (London: Thomas Richardson, 1866), p. 362.
2. David Cannadine, "War and death, grief and mourning in modern Britain", in J. Whaley (ed.), *Mirrors of Mortality: Studies in the Social History of Death* (London: Europa, 1981), p. 191.
3. This phenomenon is well described in James Stevens Curl, *The Victorian Celebration of Death* (Newton Abbot: David & Charles, 1972).
4. Philippe Ariès, *Western Attitudes Toward Death: From the Middle Ages to the Present* (London: Johns Hopkins University Press, 1976). See also Philippe Ariès, *The Hour of Our Death* (New York: Knopf, 1981).
5. William Benham, *Catharine and Crauford Tait: A Memoir* (London: Macmillan, 1879), p. 290.
6. Benham, *Catharine and Crauford Tait*, p. 299.
7. Benham, *Catharine and Crauford Tait*, pp. 327 and 390.
8. On this, see Pat Jalland, *Death in the Victorian Family* (Oxford: Oxford University Press, 1996), pp. 81–93.
9. John Morley, *Death, Heaven and the Victorians* (London: Studio Vista, 1971), p. 106. The popularity of spiritualism in Victorian Britain and its impact on clergy is well described in Georgina Byrne, "Angels Seen Today: The Theology of Modern Spiritualism and Its Impact on Church of England Clergy, 1852–1939", in Peter Clarke and Tony Claydon (eds), *The Church, The Afterlife and the Fate of the Soul* (Woodbridge: Boydell Press, 2009), pp. 360–70.
10. Geoffrey Rowell, *Hell and the Victorians: A Study of the Nineteenth-century Theological Controversies concerning Eternal Punishment and the Future Life* (Oxford: Clarendon Press, 1974), p. 22.
11. Jalland, *Death in the Victorian Family*, p. 269.
12. Benham, *Catharine and Crauford Tait*, p. 344.
13. See B. Parsons, *Committed to the Cleansing Flames: The Development of Creation in Nineteenth-Century England* (Reading: Spire Books, 2005).
14. Rowell, *Hell and the Victorians*, p. 3.
15. Lewis Richard Farnell, *An Oxonian Looks Back* (London: Martin Hopkinson, 1934), pp. 26–7. I owe these references to my friend John Winckler.

16 Rowell, *Hell and the Victorians*, pp. 147–8.
17 John Stuart Mill, *An Examination of Sir William Hamilton's Philosophy*, 6th edn (London: Longmans, Green, 1889), p. 129.
18 Rowell, *Hell and the Victorians*, p. 123.
19 Rowell, *Hell and the Victorians*, p. 118.
20 Rowell, *Hell and the Victorians*, p. 215.
21 Jalland, *Death in the Victorian Family*, p. 266
22 Bernhard Lang, *Meeting in Heaven: Modernising the Christian Afterlife 1600–2000* (Oxford: Peter Lang, 2011), p. 153.
23 Ian Bradley, *The Quiet Haven: An Anthology of Readings on Death and Heaven* (London: Darton, Longman & Todd, 2021), p. 56.
24 William Branks, *Heaven our Home: We have no saviour but Jesus, and no home but Heaven* (Edinburgh: William Nimmo, 1861), p. 12, italics in the original.
25 Branks, *Heaven our Home*, p. iii, italics in the original.
26 Michael Ledger-Lomas, *Queen Victoria: This Thorny Crown* (Oxford: Oxford University Press, 2021), p. 209.
27 Walter Walsh, *The Religious Life and Influence of Queen Victoria* (London: Swan Sonnenschein & Co., 1902), p. 184.
28 Walsh, *The Religious Life and Influence of Queen Victoria*, p. 125.
29 *Queen Victoria's Journal*, 31 May 1863, Vol. 52, p. 201 at <http://www.queenvictoriasjournals.org/search/displayItemFromId.do?FormatType=fulltextimgsrc&QueryType=articles&ItemID=18630531>, accessed 9 March 2023.
30 *Services held in Windsor Castle, on the Anniversary of the Lamented Death of the Prince Consort* (Oxford, 1862), pp. 13–16.
31 James Fleming, *Personal Recognition in Eternity: A Sermon Preached Before their Royal Highnesses the Prince and Princess of Wales, in Sandringham Church, on Sunday Morning, January 24th, 1892* (London: Skeffington & Son, 1892), pp. 7–8.
32 Ledger-Lomas, *Queen Victoria*, p. 214.

# 1

# "There is a happy land, far, far away"

## Hymns about heaven

For the last 200 years and more, hymns have been the principal vehicle for the transmission of theology and doctrine both to the great majority of churchgoers and to the general population. This was pre-eminently true in the Victorian age, the period when hymn singing was widely adopted in the Church of England and the Church of Scotland, both of which had hitherto spurned it as a dangerously over-emotional, enthusiastic and subjective practice suitable only for dissenting sects. Hymn books rolled off the presses, selling in their tens of thousands. The British Library catalogue of printed books lists over 1200 hymn books published between 1837 and 1901. Hymns were sung not just in church services and Sunday school classes but in school assemblies, at home, in the streets and in social, public and political gatherings. In my book *Abide With Me: The World of Victorian Hymns*, I liken them to television soap operas today in terms of their pervasive cultural influence and impact. They became deeply embedded in popular consciousness and profoundly shaped faith and belief across all classes and generations.

So if we want an insight into Victorian views about heaven, hymns are a good place to begin. There is certainly no shortage of them on the subject. Heaven is one of the favourite themes of Victorian hymnwriters from across the theological and denominational spectrum, High, Low and Broad Church, Anglican, Nonconformist and Roman Catholic. As we have already noted, it is the subject of over 100 hymns in the 1889 edition of the Anglican *Hymns Ancient & Modern*, the bestselling hymn book of the age—so great was the demand for this particular edition that one million copies were dispatched by the publishers on the day of publication. It is also a very popular theme in Nonconformist hymnals, many of which devote substantial sub-sections to it. The 1898 *Church Hymnary*, the main hymn book for the Church of Scotland and the Presbyterian churches in England, Ireland, Wales and across the Empire, contains 15 hymns grouped under the heading "Heavenly Glory" and a further 11 specifically for young people in a section simply entitled "Heaven".

Two hymns which date respectively from the year before and the year after the Queen's accession and which both became hugely popular throughout her reign set the tone for the Victorian hymnological treatment of heaven. The first, written by Thomas Taylor, a Congregationalist minister in Bradford, as he lay dying and published in 1836, appeared in over 600 hymnals:

> I'm but a stranger here,
> Heaven is my home;
> Earth is a desert drear;
> Heaven is my home:
> Danger and sorrow stand
> Round me on every hand;
> Heaven is my fatherland,
> Heaven is my home.
>
> There at my Saviour's side,
> Heaven is my home;
> I shall be glorified,
> Heaven is my home.
> There are the good and blest,
> Those I love most and best;
> And there I too shall rest,
> Heaven is my home.

Therefore I murmur not,
Heaven is my home;
Whate'er my earthly lot,
Heaven is my home:
And I shall surely stand
There at my Lord's right hand:
Heaven is my fatherland,
Heaven is my home.

The second hymn, written and published in 1838 by Andrew Young, an Edinburgh schoolmaster, was only slightly less popular, going on to appear in over 560 hymn books by the end of the century:

There is a happy land, far, far away,
Where saints in glory stand, bright, bright as day;
Oh, how they sweetly sing, worthy is our Saviour King,
Loud let His praises ring, praise, praise for aye.

Come to that happy land, come, come away;
Why will you doubting stand, why still delay?
Oh, we shall happy be, when from sin and sorrow free,
Lord, we shall live with Thee, blest, blest for aye.

Bright, in that happy land, beams every eye;
Kept by a Father's hand, love cannot die;
Oh, then to glory run; be a crown and kingdom won;
And, bright, above the sun, we reign for aye.

Several themes that are prominent in these two hymns recur again and again in Victorian hymnody. Perhaps the most ubiquitous is the idea of heaven as home, which is particularly marked in Taylor's hymn and which drew its scriptural warrant from such texts as Hebrews 13:14 (KJV): "For here we have no continuing city, but we seek the one to come." Among the prominent hymnwriters who took it up were Henry Baker, vicar of Monkland, Herefordshire and editor of *Hymns Ancient & Modern*, in "There is a blessed home beyond this land of woe/where trials never come, nor tears of sorrow flow" (1861) and John Mason Neale, the Tractarian priest who translated so many of the Greek and Latin hymns of the early church, in "Safe home, safe home in port" (1862). Neale's "Jerusalem the Golden", based on verses by Bernard of Cluny, with its line "O sweet and blessed country, the home of God's elect", made its way into over 850 hymn books and was a particular favourite of Queen Victoria. The Free Church of Scotland's *Home and School Hymnal* (1897) was by no means unusual in heading its selection of funeral hymns "Homecoming".

This theme was equally popular on the other side of the Atlantic. The image of going home to heaven is prominent in the *Sacred Harp Hymnal* of 1844, born out of the singing schools of New England and the shape note tradition that became so important in the American South in the later nineteenth century. It also occurs in many of the African American spirituals of this period. "Swing low, sweet chariot,/Coming for to carry me home", which was written in the mid-1860s by Wallis Willis, a freed slave, draws its inspiration from the story of Elijah being taken up to heaven in a chariot in 2 Kings 2. "Deep River", dating from the same period, contains the line "My home is over Jordan". The portrayal of heaven as home is especially clear in a hymn written in 1868 by De Witt Huntington, a minister in the US Methodist Episcopal Church, which became very popular in Evangelical churches and gospel halls in Britain:

> O think of the home over there,
> By the side of the river of light,
> Where the saints, all immortal and fair,
> Are robed in their garments of white.
>
> O think of the friends over there,
> Who before us the journey have trod;
> Of the song that they breathe on the air
> In their home in the palace of God.

> I'll soon be at home over there,
> For the end of the journey I see;
> Many dear to my heart over there
> Are watching and waiting for me.

Closely associated with this view of heaven as home was a firm conviction that friends and family would meet and be reunited there, as clearly expressed in the last verse of De Witt Huntington's hymn above, and in the lines, "There are the good and blest/Those I love most and best" in Thomas Taylor's "I'm but a stranger here". This promise recurs in many Victorian hymns, perhaps most beautifully and poetically in "Ten thousand times ten thousand", written in 1867 by Henry Alford when Dean of Canterbury Cathedral:

> O then what raptured greetings
> On Canaan's happy shore!
> What knitting severed friendships up,
> Where partings are no more!
> Then eyes with joy shall sparkle
> That brimmed with tears of late,
> Orphans no longer fatherless,
> Nor widows desolate.

A rather more tentative and plaintive note on this subject is struck in one of the most popular hymns of Mary Ann Hearn, the prolific Baptist writer and teacher who wrote under the pseudonym Marianne Farningham. The refrain of "When my final farewell to the world I have said" repeatedly asks whether anyone will be watching and waiting for her when and if she gets to heaven, and in the last verse she reflects somewhat ruefully:

> Methinks I should mourn o'er my sinful neglect,
> If sorrow in heaven could be,
> Should no one I love at the beautiful gate,
> Be waiting and watching for me.

Another popular theme which is very clearly conveyed in the first line of Andrew Young's hymn is of heaven as a happy land. It resonated with much Victorian thinking about the afterlife, as expressed in Tennyson's question, "How fares it with the happy dead?", and extended across the denominational spectrum. This idea had been expressed in the eighteenth century, most memorably by Isaac Watts in "There is a land of pure delight where saints immortal reign", but it was in the nineteenth century that it really took off. One of its earliest expressions is in this hymn written in 1809 by the Evangelical Irish preacher Thomas Kelly:

> Hark! a voice, it cries from heaven,
> Happy in the Lord who die:
> Happy they to whom 'tis given,
> From a world of grief to fly!

In 1834, Henry Francis Lyte, perpetual curate of Lower Brixham, Devon, now best remembered as the author of 'Abide With Me", wrote, "Pleasant are Thy courts above/In the land of light and love" with its wonderful affirmation:

> Happy birds that sing and fly
> Round Thy altars, O Most High;
> Happier souls that find a rest
> In a heavenly Father's breast!

Two hymns written in 1862 pursue this theme: "Saviour, blessed saviour" by the Anglican priest, Godfrey Thring, portrays heaven as a place "Where no pain nor sorrow/Toil nor care is known", while Frederick William Faber asks the rhetorical question, "Who would not seek the happy land/Where they that loved are blest?" in "O Paradise! O Paradise".

Similar imagery is found in Gospel songs. William Hunter's "We're bound for the land of the pure and the holy", first published in 1845, describes heaven as "the home of the happy, the kingdom of love" and promises:

No poverty there, no, the saints are all wealthy,
The heirs of His glory whose nature is love;
No sickness can reach them, that country is healthy;
O say, will you go to the Eden above?

Both Taylor's "I'm but a stranger here" and Young's "There is a happy land" give heaven a distinct geographical, or perhaps more precisely cosmological, location, in Young's words both "far, far away" and "bright, above the sun". Despite scientific advances and biblical criticism, what is being offered in these and other hymns is a very literal and primitive view of heaven as a realm high up in the skies. They also convey a very clear sense that the inhabitants of heaven will be in close proximity to Jesus, in Taylor's words, "There at my Saviour's side". Both hymns have more than a whiff of universalism and a sense that everyone will get to heaven. This is surely the message of Young's confident assertion that "Bright, in that happy land, beams every eye". Neither makes any mention of hell, nor do most of the hymns that followed them.

There is a slight difference of emphasis in these two hymns which to some extent express two competing views of heaven in the Victorian mind. Taylor's is more individualistic—the first-person singular pronoun is used throughout and the emphasis is on heaven as "my home", the rest I shall find there and the friends and family with whom I shall be united. In this respect, it is strongly anthropocentric and it introduces a major theme in Victorian hymns about heaven—and in more general thinking—that heaven will be an extension of life on earth with a similar emphasis on home, family and relationships. Young's is more communal—with the first-person plural being used throughout—and it is also more theocentric. With its picture of the saints sweetly singing praise to God, it conveys more of a sense of heaven as a place of worship.

Later Victorian hymnwriters painted more elaborate pictures of heaven than the relatively unsophisticated and simple portrayals by Taylor and Young, while continuing to describe it in highly traditional and ethereal terms. Descriptions of white-robed angels strumming harps and singing unceasingly were particularly, although not exclusively, popular with High Churchmen, as in this hymn written by J. M. Neale in 1842:

> Around the throne of God a band
> Of glorious angels ever stand;
> Bright things they see, sweet harps they hold,
> And on their heads are crowns of gold.

Similar imagery was enthusiastically invoked by Francis Potts in 1861 with his "Angel voices ever singing round Thy throne of light,/Angel harps, forever ringing, rest not day nor night" and Henry Alford in his "Ten thousand times ten thousand" (1867) with the "ringing of a thousand harps". J. M. Neale was particularly keen on this kind of imagery and on portraying heaven first and foremost as a place of worship. He also emphasized its hierarchical status while wanting to maintain at the same time that all dwelling there were engaged together in the single task of glorifying God. His hymn "Our Father's home eternal", very loosely based on verses by Thomas à Kempis, goes through the various classes "among the happy number" who inhabit heaven, beginning with the Virgin Mary, the patriarchs and prophets, continuing with the apostles, martyrs, virgins and confessors and "the holy men and women, their earthly struggle o'er", and ending with:

> And every faithful servant
> Made perfect in Thy grace,
> Hath each his fitting station
> 'Mid those that see Thy face;
> The bondsman and the noble,
> The peasant and the king,
> All gird one glorious Monarch
> In one eternal ring.

The image of heaven as a happy home with a distinct location above the sky where friends and family will be reunited and white-robed saints continually sing their praises to God was carried over into many hymns written specifically for children. Death and dying featured prominently in Victorian children's hymns, often being portrayed in graphic terms with harrowing descriptions of "the feeble pulse, the gasping breath/the clenched teeth, the glazed eye". Undoubtedly they frightened many of those who sang them, as they did Janet Hogarth, the journalist daughter of a Lincolnshire vicar, who forever connected hymns with the fear of death. Other clerical children had a very different attitude to them. In her final hours, Mary (May), the last of Catharine and Archibald Tait's children to die, requested to have read to her Thomas Kelly's hymn, "Away, thou dying saint, away./Fly to the mansions of the blest". Her mother noted, "She had found it for herself; and almost always in health, this dear girl would find and choose a hymn about death."[1] Another favourite with the Tait children was Henry Milman's "Brother, thou art gone before us", which as well as being an anthem was also a popular hymn promising reunion with "the good" in heaven (see p. 15).

In the early part of the nineteenth century, there were children's hymns about hell, principally designed to inculcate moral values and good behaviour, and often pretty crude, like the one that appeared in a hymn book issued in 1831 by the National Society, the body that supervised all Church of England schools:

> Children, never tell a lie:
> Don't you know that when you die,
> God for every lie you tell,
> May remove your soul to Hell?

As the century progressed, however, mentions of hell in children's hymns, as elsewhere, became increasingly few and far between. Heaven, by contrast, featured more and more prominently. It is the subject of by far the longest subsection of "Hymns for the Young" in the 1898 *Church Hymnary*, the main hymn book for the Church of Scotland and Presbyterian churches in England, Ireland, Wales and across the Empire. Many show a strong pastoral concern in the face of the high infant and child mortality rates which took so many children suddenly away from their parents and siblings. They provide reassurance that those who die young go to a better place and a happier life. A similar emphasis to that found in adult hymns on the reuniting of friends and family and a similar universalist tendency combine with a didactic desire to teach the doctrine of eternal life and also the moral lesson that those who are good will go there.

Several of these themes—notably the inculcation of faith and good behaviour, the pastoral concern and the assurance of meeting up with friends—in this case, teachers and pastors—are prominent in "Here we suffer grief and pain" written by Thomas Bilby, principal of teacher training colleges in London and the West Indies, which was first published in 1832 and set to the tune JOYFUL. It was a favourite hymn for Victorian children to be taught to memorize. Ten-year-old Catherine (Catty) Tait chose it to sing with her siblings following the death of her younger sister Charlotte. In Thomas Hardy's novel *Tess of the D'Urbervilles*, Tess' young brother, Abraham, learns it at his National (i.e. Church of England) School:

> Here we suffer grief and pain;
> Here we meet to part again;
> In heaven we part no more.
>
> All who love the Lord below,
> When they die, to heaven shall go,
> And sing with Saints above.
>
> Little children will be there,
> Who have sought the Lord in prayer,
> From every Sabbath school.
>
> Teachers, too, shall meet above,
> And our pastors, whom we love,
> Shall meet to part no more.

The prospect of being reunited with teachers was not universally appealing. In the world of improving fiction, pious children might repeat these verses on their death beds, as in Julia Mathews' 1855 novel *Alice Gray*, but in real life they came in for rather less reverential treatment, as in this version sung by the boys of one Yorkshire village:

> Here we suffer grief and pain—
> Over the road they're doing the same,
> Next door they're suffering more;
> Oh, won't it be joyful when we part to meet no more.

The dual sense of heaven as a reward for those who love God in this world and a place where people will be reunited after death is strongly conveyed in several of the most popular and enduring Victorian children's hymns. They also give it a precise, almost concrete location and paint a picture of a happy home packed with happy children, perhaps most famously in "I think when I read that sweet story of old", written in 1841 by Jemima Luke to go with a Greek air which had captivated her by its pathos when she heard it played while visiting an infant school in Gray's Inn Road, London. It went on to appear in nearly 800 hymnals. This hymn has a decidedly universalist feel, certainly in terms of preaching a doctrine of universal rather than limited atonement in its concluding verses:

> But thousands and thousands who wander and fall,
> never heard of that heavenly home;
> I wish they could know there is room for them all,
> and that Jesus has bid them to come.
>
> In that beautiful place he has gone to prepare
> for all who are washed and forgiven;
> and many dear children shall be with him there,
> for 'of such is the kingdom of heaven'.
>
> I long for the joy of that glorious time,
> the sweetest and brightest and best,
> when the dear little children of every clime
> shall crowd to his arms and be blest.

Almost as popular was "There's a Friend for Little Children", written in 1859 by Albert Midlane, an ironmonger on the Isle of Wight, which appeared in over 220 hymnals with its comforting affirmation:

> There's a home for little children
> Above the bright blue sky,
> Where Jesus reigns in glory,
> A home of peace and joy.
> No home on earth is like it,
> Or can with it compare,
> For every one is happy
> Nor could be happier there.

Similar imagery is found in Emily Elliott's "There came a little child to earth":

> Far away in the goodly land
> Fair and bright;
> Children with crowns of glory stand,
> Robed in white.

Significantly, very few hymns for children or adults mention judgment or the Resurrection, or refer to a period of sleep or limbo between death and heaven. Most rather imply a relatively swift and effortless passage to the next world, especially for children, often facilitated by an angel, and display a strong preference for the doctrine of the immortality of the soul over that of the resurrection of the body. Typical is the sentiment expressed in "The Apostle Slept", written in 1858 by the Free Church of Scotland minister, James Drummond Burns:

> So when the Christian's eyelid droops and closes
> In nature's parting strife,
> A friendly Angel stands where he reposes,
> To wake him up to life.
>
> He gives a gentle blow, and so releases
> The spirit from its clay;
> From sin's temptations, and from life's distresses,
> He bids it to come away.

Some hymn books did provide hymns dealing with the doctrine of resurrection. The 1887 *Congregational Hymnal* includes separate sections on "Death", "The Rest after Death", "The Resurrection" and "The Final Glory of Heaven". The *Church Hymnary* of 1898 similarly has separate sections entitled "Death and Resurrection" and "Heavenly Glory", with 15 hymns in each. The former section includes three hymns, "Asleep in Jesus!", "Sleep on, beloved, sleep" and "Sleep thy last sleep", which focus on the period between death and the Day of Resurrection. The first of these, written in 1832 by Margaret Mackay, the daughter of an army officer, and also the wife of one, and published in over 1000 hymnals, combines an atmosphere of peace and calm with a clear sense of the Resurrection, although it is the former which clearly predominates:

> Asleep in Jesus! blessed sleep,
> From which none ever wakes to weep!
> A calm and undisturbed repose,
> Unbroken by the last of foes.
>
> Asleep in Jesus! O for me
> May such a blissful refuge be!
> Securely shall my ashes lie,
> waiting the summons from on high.

Two of the most prolific and popular Anglican hymnwriters, Sabine Baring-Gould and Christopher Wordsworth, penned verses which imaginatively expounded the difficult doctrine of bodily resurrection ("On the Resurrection Morning/Soul and body meet again" and "Alleluia, Alleluia, Hearts to Heaven and voices raise" respectively). But significantly these were put in the "Easter" section of hymn books and, like other hymns about the Resurrection, tended to be applied primarily to Jesus and used at Easter rather than sung at funerals.

Clerical attempts were made to suppress the popular funeral anthems sung by mourners at the graves of their loved ones which suggested the soul flying out of the body and being instantly liberated and carried to heaven. The most popular of these, "The Vital Spark", an ode by Alexander Pope, climbed to the top of the west gallery pop chart largely on the basis of its jaunty fuguing tune by Edward Harwood. These anthems gradually disappeared through the nineteenth century, largely thanks to changes in musical taste and church music repertoire with the disappearance of the west gallery bands in favour of robed choirs, rather than because of any diminution of the popular belief in immortality over resurrection. As Brian Castle observes on the basis of his exhaustive study of the treatment of the Four Last Things in Victorian hymns, "There was a preference for the immortality of the soul rather than the resurrection of the body in the Victorian understanding of the afterlife."[2]

At the very end of the nineteenth century, the proprietors of *Hymns Ancient & Modern* took a stand against certain hymns which seemed to argue that some Christians bypassed the normal process of dying and rising again on the Day of Resurrection by going straight to heaven. Curiously, they did not object to those of impeccable evangelical pedigree, including classic eighteenth-century hymns like Isaac Watts' "There is a land of pure delight" and Charles Wesley's "Let Saints on earth in concert sing", but to the more recent Catholic-inclined hymns which suggested a direct ascent to heaven on the part of the saints. Two of the hymns in the supplementary section of the 1889 hymnal for "Burial of the Dead" particularly concerned the compilers: J. M. Neale's immensely popular "Safe home, safe home in port", with its reassuring couplet "The lamb is in the fold,/In perfect safety penn'd", and Henrietta Dobree's "Safely, safely gather'd in".

When word got round in 1897 that the compilers were considering dropping these hymns from the next edition, there was a concerted protest from High Church clergy, who threatened to change to another hymn book if these "radical changes in a Protestant direction" were made. The compilers responded characteristically by setting up a high-powered committee "upon hymns on heaven and kindred subjects". After taking soundings from a number of theologians, it concluded that

> there is no scriptural warrant for assuming that any of the departed Saints are risen or will rise from the dead before the General Resurrection at the Last Day; or that it is possible for human beings to enter into full fruition of heavenly blessedness without the Resurrection of the Body. We should not wish,

therefore, to see the book include any hymns which appear distinctly to teach the contrary.³

Both of the offending hymns were dropped from the next edition of *Hymns Ancient & Modern*, which appeared in 1904, although they were brought back again in the "Complete Edition" two years later. The fact was that, overwhelmingly, it was hymns about heaven rather than the intermediate state or the general resurrection that might precede it after death that Victorian hymnwriters wanted to write about and Victorian congregations wanted to sing.

Behind this tendency towards universalism, emphasis on immortality rather than resurrection, lack of focus on judgment, and portrayal of heaven as a happy and homely land where friends would be united lay a strong pastoral impulse. Victorian hymnwriters, a good number of whom were parish clergy dealing on an almost daily basis with the dying and the grieving, sought to offer consolation and comfort to those going through the pain of bereavement, and especially the loss of children. Victorian hymns are often accused of being sentimental and appealing to the heart rather than the head, but there was a very good pastoral reason for their emphasis on heaven as home and a place of rest where family and friends would meet again and angelic choirs sing.

## Notes

[1] William Benham, *Catharine and Crauford Tait: A Memoir* (London: Macmillan, 1879), p. 372.
[2] Brian Castle, *Sing A New Song to the Lord* (London: Darton, Longman & Todd, 1994), p. 35.
[3] *Report of the Sub-Committee on Hymns on Heaven and Kindred Subjects*, Hymns Ancient & Modern archives, Norwich, 1897.

2

# "How fares it with the happy dead?"

*Alfred Tennyson*

For Alfred Tennyson (1809–92), whose forty-plus-year reign as Poet Laureate from 1850 to 1892 confirmed his status as the Victorians' favourite poet, life after death was "the cardinal point of Christianity".[1] It could not be a matter of absolute certainty but "if faith means anything at all, it is trusting to those instincts, or feelings, or whatever they may be called, which assure us of some life after this".[2] In a conversation with the Queen he went further, saying that "if there is no immortality of the soul, one does not see why there should be any God . . . you cannot love a Father who strangled you".[3] Indeed, it is not too much to say that belief in a future life was the substance and pretty well the sum total of his religious belief. "There's something that watches over us", he once remarked, "and our individuality endures. That's my faith and that's all my faith."[4]

Tennyson wrote most extensively and famously about death and what may lie beyond it in his long poem *In Memoriam*, the 723 verses of which were composed over a period of 17 years following the death of his great friend Arthur Hallam at the age of 22 in 1833. Published in 1850, it almost certainly had more impact and influence than anything else written on the subject in the nineteenth century, helping to establish and confirm the hopeful if not certain view of heaven that was so widely held, especially by liberal Protestants. Indeed, as Michael Wheeler puts it, "Tennyson came to be seen as the laureate of the Broad Church."[5] Frederick Robertson, the Anglican clergyman who became one of the most famous and widely followed preachers in Britain during his six years as incumbent at Holy Trinity, Brighton, before his death at the age of 37 in 1853, felt that *In Memoriam* contained "the *most* satisfactory things that have ever been said on the future state".⁶ F. D. Maurice dedicated his *Theological Essays* to Tennyson in gratitude for it and Frederic Farrar's *Mercy and Judgment*, which argued against the doctrine of eternal punishment, carried a similar dedication.

Queen Victoria was particularly affected by *In Memoriam* She read it often in the aftermath of the death of her beloved husband, Prince Albert, in 1861, marking verses that brought particular comfort and copying extracts into her *Album Inconsolativum*, a manuscript anthology of mourning verses. When the Duke of Argyll visited her at Osborne House in 1862, she told him how it had confirmed "the reality of her belief in the *Life Presence* of the dead", reinforced her conviction that she would meet Albert again in heaven and validated her dislike of the word "late" being applied to him.⁷ After meeting Tennyson at Osborne House in 1883 she noted in her journal that:

> he talked of the many friends he had lost, and what would be if we did not feel and know there was another world, where there would be no partings; And then he spoke of his horror of the unbelievers and philosophers who would make you believe that there was *no* other world, no Immortality—who tried to explain *all* away in a miserable manner. We agreed that were such a thing possible, God, who is love, would be far more cruel than any human being.⁸

*In Memoriam* is in large part a eulogy and lament for Hallam and a reflection on grieving as the author expresses his intense feelings over the loss of his fellow poet and intimate friend. But the mood gradually changes from despair to hope and there are significant passages which explore the possibility of an afterlife and seek to describe what it might be like. The tone is tentative throughout and that was and is a large part of the poem's appeal. There is no blind dogmatic certainty resting on the Church's teaching, a literalist reading of the Bible or a fundamentalist theology. Rather, Tennyson bases his hope of life after death on his overwhelming sense of God's love and his conviction that it cannot be confined just to this life but must surely extend beyond the grave, as stated in the third verse of the prologue:

> Thou wilt not leave us in the dust:
> Thou madest man, he knows not why,
> He thinks he was not made to die;
> And thou hast made him: thou art just.

This is a theme that recurs again and again. Tennyson returns to it after recounting and reflecting on the biblical story of the raising of Lazarus and specifically on the faith of Mary, responding to the restoration of her brother's life with "her early Heaven, her happy views":

> My own dim life should teach me this,
> That life shall live for evermore,
> Else earth is darkness at the core,
> And dust and ashes all that is.

It is most powerfully and famously stated in stanzas 54 and 55 towards the middle of the poem:

> Oh yet we trust that somehow good
> Will be the final goal of ill,
> To pangs of nature, sins of will,
> Defects of doubt, and taints of blood;
>
> That nothing walks with aimless feet;
> That not one life shall be destroy'd,
> Or cast as rubbish to the void,
> When God hath made the pile complete;
>
> That not a worm is cloven in vain;
> That not a moth with vain desire
> Is shrivell'd in a fruitless fire,
> Or but subserves another's gain.

Behold, we know not anything;
I can but trust that good shall fall
At last—far off—at last, to all,
And every winter change to spring.

So runs my dream: but what am I?
An infant crying in the night:
An infant crying for the light:
And with no language but a cry.

The wish, that of the living whole
No life may fail beyond the grave,
Derives it not from what we have
The likest God within the soul?

Are God and Nature then at strife,
That Nature lends such evil dreams?
So careful of the type she seems,
So careless of the single life;

That I, considering everywhere
Her secret meaning in her deeds,
And finding that of fifty seeds
She often brings but one to bear,

I falter where I firmly trod,
And falling with my weight of cares
Upon the great world's altar-stairs
That slope thro' darkness up to God,

I stretch lame hands of faith, and grope,
And gather dust and chaff, and call
To what I feel is Lord of all,
And faintly trust the larger hope.

Here is the nub of Tennyson's position, which is not an argument based on evidence, but a tentative hope, based on stretching out the "lame hands of faith", and qualified by his concern about the costly waste of evolution. He expressed it clearly in prose as well as in verse:

> Is all this trouble of life worth undergoing if we only end in our own corpse-coffins at last? If you allow God, and God allows this strong instinct and universal yearning for another life, surely that is in a measure a presumption of its truth. We cannot give up the mighty hopes that make us men.[9]

When *In Memoriam* moves from the question of whether there is life after death to what it might be like if that larger hope is to be trusted, however faintly, it is equally tentative and full of allusions and further questions. Relatively early on comes an evocation of that theme found in so much Victorian writing, and discussed in Chapter 9, of the dead forming the compost out of which new life comes:

> 'Tis well; 'tis something; we may stand
> Where he in English earth is laid,
> And from his ashes may be made
> The violet of his native land.

But Tennyson's musings go far beyond noting this rather specific and short-term physical immortality whereby the dead live on in organic matter providing the material for new life. They become increasingly suffused with a kind of optimism, tentative though it is, as expressed in the question "How fares it with the happy dead?" and its answer, expressed in hope and trust, "that those we call the dead are breathers of an ampler day for ever nobler ends".

There is a moving evocation of the common motif that death is a kind of sleep in stanza 43:

> If Sleep and Death be truly one,
> And every spirit's folded bloom
> Thro' all its intervital gloom
> In some long trance should slumber on;
>
> Unconscious of the sliding hour,
> Bare of the body, might it last,
> And silent traces of the past
> Be all the colour of the flower:
>
> So then were nothing lost to man;
> So that still garden of the souls
> In many a figured leaf enrolls
> The total world since life began;

This understanding of death as a long slumber or trance, "a garden of souls" in which all the world's life is somehow enfolded, is reinforced in stanza 58 where sleep is described as "death's twin brother".

There are several mystical passages which represent the passage to heaven in the familiar imagery of a boat crossing the sea, something that Tennyson would come back to in his poem "Crossing the Bar". In stanza 103, he has a dream of the dead Hallam standing on the deck of a great ship in the middle of the ocean. He boards the ship to join him, accompanied by a group of maidens:

> And while the wind began to sweep
> A music out of sheet and shroud,
> We steer'd her toward a crimson cloud
> That landlike slept along the deep.

Tennyson later explained that the maidens were "the Muses, poetry, arts—all that made life beautiful here, which we hope will pass with us beyond the grave".[10]

In another mystical passage in stanza 84, he meditates on what might have happened had Hallam lived longer and the two friends been taken up to heaven together as a single soul:

> Thy spirit should fail from off the globe;
>
> What time mine own might also flee,
> As link'd with thine in love and fate,
> And, hovering o'er the dolorous strait
> To the other shore, involved in thee,
>
> Arrive at last the blessed goal,
> And He that died in Holy Land
> Would reach us out the shining hand,
> And take us as a single soul.

This passage, one of the few which actually references Jesus' death and pictures Christ reaching out a hand to lead people into heaven, presents the striking image of the two friends entering heaven as "a single soul".

Like many of his contemporaries, Tennyson displayed a certain ambiguity and agnosticism in tackling the question as to whether we retain our individual identities and personalities in the next life or rather become merged and absorbed into some wider, more amorphous, divine whole. He wrote of often having a "waking trance" in which his own individuality "seemed to dissolve and fade away into boundless being" with "the loss of personality seeming no extinction but the only true life" and pondered if this is the state that St Paul describes in 1 Corinthians 15.[11] However, he told his son, Hallam, "If the absorption into the divine in the after-life be the creed of some, let them at all events allow us many existences of individuality before this absorption; since this short-lived individuality seems to be but too short a preparation for so mighty a union." After quoting this in his *Memoir*, Hallam went on to say that his father held that "each individual will had a spiritual and eternal significance with relation to their individual wills as well as to the Supreme and Eternal Will".[12] *In Memoriam* comes down firmly in favour of the retention of the individual personality after death:

> That each, who seems a separate whole,
> Should move his rounds, and fusing all
> The skirts of self again, should fall
> Remerging in the general Soul,
>
> Is faith as vague as all unsweet:
> Eternal form shall still divide
> The eternal soul from all beside;
> And I shall know him when we meet:
>
> And we shall sit at endless feast,
> Enjoying each the other's good:
> What vaster dream can hit the mood
> Of Love on earth?

It is telling that it is the prospect of being reunited with Hallam, knowing him again and sitting together at the heavenly banquet, that leads Tennyson to his conclusion that "Eternal form shall still divide/The eternal soul from all beside". It is also telling that while acknowledging this is ultimately a dream rather than a certainty, he grounds it on the reality of God's love as it is shown here on earth.

Alongside this belief that our individual personalities endure beyond death is a strong sense that, along with God, the dead watch over us and look down on our human foibles and weaknesses with pity and compassion. Stanza 51 begins "The dead shall look me thro and thro" and continues:

> Be near us when we climb or fall:
> Ye watch, like God, the rolling hours
> With larger other eyes than ours,
> To make allowance for us all.

At her first meeting with Tennyson in 1862, Queen Victoria told him that those couplets had been of particular comfort to her. They convey a message similar to that articulated so clearly in Frederick William Faber's hymn "There's a wideness in God's mercy", with its statement that "There is no place where earth's sorrows are more keenly felt than heaven" (p. 87).

*In Memoriam* portrays "the long harmonious years" of death in terms of activity and progress rather than static rest. Tennyson writes of heaven, "For here the man is more and more", and conveys a similar sense of it as a realm of human progress in the already quoted lines "Those we call the dead are breathers of an ampler day for ever nobler ends". In stanza 40, he says of the dead Hallam:

> And, doubtless, unto thee is given
> A life that bears immortal fruit
> In those great offices that suit
> The full-grown energies of heaven.

These "full-grown energies of heaven" are never explored or explained but there is more than a hint here of the strenuous, exhilarating afterlife as imagined by F. D. Maurice, William Ellery Channing, Benjamin Jowett and others and discussed in Chapters 6 and 10. Stanza 82 is even more explicit about the progressive nature of the afterlife and invokes the image of the chrysalis to suggest the change and transformation that occurs in it:

> Eternal process moving on,
> From state to state the spirit walks;
> And these are but the shatter'd stalks,
> Or ruin'd chrysalis of one.

Tennyson returns to this theme in his 1892 poem "The Death of the Duke of Clarence and Avondale", where he writes of death:

> His truer name
> Is 'Onward', no discordance in the roll
> And march of that Eternal Harmony
> Whereto the worlds beat time, tho' faintly heard
> Until the great Hereafter.

Despite its opening line, "Strong Son of God, Immortal Love", there is little about Jesus in "In Memoriam" and virtually nothing about his Resurrection, nor indeed about resurrection more generally. The story of Lazarus is referenced not for the miracle of the rising of the dead man but for what it says about the faith of his sister Mary. There is much more of an emphasis on the birth of Christ, reflected in the significance attached to the three Christmases mentioned in the poem, than on his death. As Michael Wheeler observes, "For Tennyson, resurrection seems to have been a less secure ground for belief in a future life than the revelation of God's love in the incarnation".[13] It is indeed the "Immortal Love" that Tennyson focuses on throughout the poem. As Frederick Robertson rightly discerned, the underlying message of "In Memoriam" is "that Love is King; that the Immortal is in us; that, which is the keynote of the whole, 'All is well, tho' Faith and Form be sundered in the night of fear'".[14]

Tennyson approaches death and immortality as a poet using imagination rather than reason, feeling rather than rational analysis, and appealing to the heart rather than the head. This was something that struck several of the poem's greatest admirers. Robertson observed that Tennyson dealt with "doubts and worse ... not as a philosopher would answer them, nor as a theologian, or a metaphysician, but as it is the duty of a poet to reply, by intuitive faculty, in strains in which Imagination predominates over Thought and Memory".[15] Frederic Farrar made a similar point when he noted that "the intuitions of the poet, like those of the Saint, may contain more essential truth than the limitless inferences of theologians from dimly apprehended metaphors".[16]

*In Memoriam* is not Alfred Tennyson's only poem to reflect on death and the afterlife, although it offers by far his most sustained, nuanced and significant treatment of the subject. In "Maud" (1855), he reflects enigmatically that

> for sullen-seeming Death may give
> More life to Love than is or ever was
> In our low world, where yet 'tis sweet to live.

Later, in "Lancelot and Elaine" from *Idylls of the King*, he has death calling "like a friend's voice from a distant field approaching through the darkness", somewhat in the manner of Adelaide Procter (p. 50).

It is in the short poem "Crossing the Bar" that he gives his other best known and often-quoted view of death and what follows it. It was written in 1889 after Tennyson had experienced a serious illness and was pondering his own mortality. Based on his familiarity with the strong tides of the Solent which he saw from his home on the Isle of Wight, it uses the imagery of crossing over the sandbar to catch the tide where a river meets the sea. The poem imagines the dying individual, like a boat, putting out to sea and crossing the bar "when that which drew from out the boundless deep turns again home". Borne by the flood from "our bourne of time and place", the dead soul hopes to see "my Pilot face to face". Tennyson later wrote: "The Pilot has been on board all the while, but in the dark I have not seen him ... [He is] that Divine and Unseen Who is always guiding us".[17] So there is a sense here of heaven as both a setting out and a homecoming, and above all as an encounter with God, the one who has always been guiding us, even though we have never seen Him.

Although "Crossing the Bar" portrays what follows death as a meeting with God, Tennyson took an essentially anthropological rather than a theological view of heaven—it is a place not primarily of worship but rather of reunion between friends and family, energetic common endeavour and progressive development. Like so many of his Broad Church contemporaries, his belief in an afterlife sprang from deep pastoral concern and sensitivity and his own lived experience. His son, Hallam, recalled him saying, "I can hardly understand how any great, imaginative man, who has deeply lived, suffered, thought and wrought, can doubt of the Soul's continuous progress in the after-life."[18]

More emphatically and unequivocally than Maurice or Farrar, Tennyson was a universalist. In his *Memoir* of his father, Hallam records that

> I have heard him say that he 'would rather know that he was to be lost eternally than not know that the whole human race was to live eternally'; and when he speaks of 'faintly trusting the larger

hope' he means by 'the larger hope' that the whole human race would through, perhaps, ages of suffering, be at length purified and saved.[19]

This universalism was similarly driven by moral and pastoral considerations which overrode traditional church teaching and the principles of dogmatic theology. As his friend Robert Bickersteth, the Bishop of Ripon, put it, Tennyson had "an irreverent impatience of formal dogma" and "a feeling that the truth must be larger, purer, nobler than any mere human expression or definition of it".[20] His lack of attention to creeds and dogma is well expressed in his remark that "it is impossible to imagine that the Almighty will ask you, when you come before Him in the next life what your particular form of creed was: but the question will rather be, 'Have you been true to yourself, and given in My Name a cup of cold water to one of these little ones?'"[21] Here we have the essence of his approach to the question of the afterlife and the basis of "the larger hope" in which he trusted, faintly or otherwise. It was at once pastoral, sentimental and practical—much like those Victorian hymns that we have already surveyed, albeit of a more literary character. It was, indeed, not surprising that stanzas from *In Memoriam* and the whole of "Crossing the Bar" found their way into numerous Victorian hymn books and became among the most popular of the many hymns about heaven.

## Notes

[1] Hallam Tennyson, *Alfred Lord Tennyson: A Memoir* (London: Macmillan, 1897), p. 321.
[2] Tennyson, *Tennyson*, p. 495.
[3] Giles St Aubyn, *Souls in Torment: Victorian Faith in Crisis* (London: Sinclair Stevenson, 2011), p. 176.
[4] St Aubyn, *Souls in Torment*, p. 203.
[5] Michael Wheeler, *Death and the Future Life in Victorian Literature and Theology* (Cambridge: Cambridge University Press, 1990), p. 228.
[6] Tennyson, *Tennyson*, p. 298.

7 Hope Dyson and Charles Tennyson (eds), *Dear and Honoured Lady: The Correspondence Between Queen Victoria and Alfred Tennyson* (London: Macmillan, 1969), p. 69.
8 Dyson and Tennyson (eds), *Dear and Honoured Lady*, p. 103.
9 Tennyson, *Tennyson*, p. 321.
10 Alfred Lord Tennyson, *In Memoriam*, eds Susan Shatto and Marion Shaw (Oxford: Oxford University Press, 1982), p. 262.
11 Tennyson, *Tennyson*, p. 320.
12 Tennyson, *Tennyson*, p. 319.
13 Wheeler, *Death and the Future Life*, p. 231.
14 Tennyson, *Tennyson*, p. 298.
15 Frederick William Robertson, *Lectures and Addresses on Literary and Social Topics* (London: Smith, Elder, 1858), pp. 125–6.
16 Wheeler, *Death and the Future Life*, p. 235.
17 Ian Bradley, *The Penguin Book of Hymns* (London: Viking, 1989), p. 369.
18 Tennyson, *Tennyson*, p. 321.
19 Tennyson, *Tennyson*, pp. 321–2.
20 Tennyson, *Tennyson*, p. 309.
21 Tennyson, *Tennyson*, p. 309.

# 3
# "I travel to meet a friend"

*Adelaide Anne Procter*

The poems of Adelaide Anne Procter (1825–64) were more widely read than those of any other Victorian writer apart from Alfred Tennyson. Reputed to be Queen Victoria's favourite versifier, she was the most published poet in *Household Words*, the popular weekly magazine edited throughout the 1850s by Charles Dickens, who became a close and admiring friend.

No one in the Victorian age wrote quite so often and so enthusiastically about death or looked forward so longingly to dying as a homecoming which would bring peace and rest from the torments and struggles of life. Many of her poems contrast the "fierce pain and pleasures dim" of this world with the lasting joys, peace and fulfilment of heaven. This theme is evident in an early poem entitled "Ministering Angels", written while she was in her teens and embracing the idea of heaven as home which we have identified in so many Victorian hymns. It concludes:

> Then leave me not alone in this bleak world,
> Where'er I roam,
> And at the end, with your bright wings unfurled,
> Oh! Take me home![1]

Procter comes back to the contrast between earth and heaven again and again, as in her poem "Life and Death", where a father, asked by his son what life is, answers that it is "a battle, where the strongest lance may fail, where the wariest eyes may be beguiled and the stoutest heart may quail". The dialogue continues:

'What is Death, Father?'
'The rest, my child,
When the strife and the toil are o'er;
The Angel of God, who, calm and mild,
Says we need fight no more;
Who, driving away the demon band,
Bids the din of the battle cease;
Takes banner and spear from our failing hand,
And proclaims an eternal Peace.'[2]

Adelaide Procter's interest in death went back to her childhood when it was commented on by contemporaries. A sickly infant, she grew up in a London literary family—her father, Bryan Procter, was a prolific poet admired by Charles Lamb and Alexander Pushkin. She was deeply affected by the death of her younger brother, Edward, who succumbed to scarlet fever at the age of six when she was nine. She herself had delicate health throughout her life and died of tuberculosis at the age of 38. At the age of 25, she converted to Roman Catholicism, and many of her poems are of a devotional nature, with a good number focused on the Virgin Mary. They often involve single young women and dwell on the themes of broken love affairs, exclusion and loneliness. Several of those which were most popular among her contemporaries are set in graveyards and crypts, like "A Tomb in Ghent", which features a "white maiden's tomb" in a cathedral crypt.

It is tempting to portray Procter as a sickly, frustrated Victorian spinster yearning for death as a release from her cramped, pain-filled, lonely and empty life, and filled with morbid thoughts and passive resignation. In fact, this was far from being the case. She was sociable and led an engaged and fulfilled life as a pioneer feminist and active philanthropist. She championed the cause of single and homeless women, serving on the committee of the Society for Promoting the Employment of Women, and was much involved in a Catholic hostel for homeless women. This active temperament was accompanied, according to Charles Dickens in his introduction to one of her many books of verse, by a cheerful and humorous disposition:

Those readers of Miss Procter's poems who should suppose from their tone that her mind was of a gloomy or despondent cast, would be curiously mistaken. She was exceedingly humorous, and had a great delight in humour. Cheerfulness was habitual with her, she was very ready at a sally or a reply, and in her laugh (as I remember well) there was an unusual vivacity, enjoyment, and sense of drollery. She was perfectly unconstrained and unaffected: as modestly silent about her productions, as she was generous with their pecuniary results. She was a friend who inspired the strongest attachments; she was a finely sympathetic woman, with a great accordant heart and a sterling noble nature.[3]

Much of Procter's poetry expresses the Christian social gospel. Her first biographer, Ferdinand Janku, suggested that the religious creed expressed in her poems is close to the Christian socialism espoused by F. D. Maurice, Charles Kingsley and others.[4] Her most recent biographer, Gill Gregory, agrees, saying that "in her poetry Procter expresses a humane and socially committed Christianity alongside a more conservative religious position advocating resignation to suffering".[5] Procter consistently argues that prayer without deeds is worthless and calls on her readers to feed the hungry and minister to the poor and homeless. The proceeds from several of her bestselling books of verse went to support a night refuge for homeless women and children in London.

Alongside this active involvement in good works, there may well also have been frustration and sadness in her private life. It appears that she was engaged to be married in her early thirties, but that her fiancé broke off the engagement suddenly, terminating a relationship that had been going on for two years. This experience may partly explain why she so often writes about the loneliness of single women, and it may also lie behind a powerful poem which she wrote in 1861, "The Story of a Faithful Soul", on the theme of Purgatory. It describes a young woman who dies the night before her wedding and longs to return from Purgatory to comfort her fiancé. The Archangel Michael grants her "one short minute's space" with her earthly lover on condition that she returns and pays for this reprieve with "a thousand years in torment". She duly returns to earth only to find that her fiancé has already remarried. On her return to Purgatory in a desolate state, she is exempted by Michael from further suffering and granted an immediate passage to heaven:

> 'Pass on,' thus spake the Angel:
> 'Heaven's joy is deep and vast;
> Pass on, pass on, poor spirit,
> For Heaven is yours at last;
> In that one minute's anguish
> Your thousand years have passed.'[6]

As well as providing an intriguing glimpse into the mid-nineteenth-century Roman Catholic understanding of Purgatory, this poem highlights Adelaide Procter's sense of heaven as a place of special reward and consolation for those who have suffered on earth.

This idea is reinforced by the way in which she portrays death as a friend, a theme brought out clearly in her poem, "A Tryst with Death":

> I am footsore and very weary,
> But I travel to meet a Friend:
> The way is long and dreary,
> But I know that it soon must end.
>
> He is travelling fast like the whirlwind,
> And though I creep slowly on,
> We are drawing nearer, nearer,
> And the journey is almost done . . .
>
> I will not fear at his coming,
> Although I must meet him alone;
> He will look in my eyes so gently,
> And take my hand in his own.
>
> Like a dream all my toil will vanish,
> When I lay my head on his breast—
> But the journey is very weary,
> And he only can give me rest![7]

This kind of longing language about death is understandable given her own increasingly painful and debilitating consumptive condition. The idea of death as a friend is by no means peculiar to Procter. We can find it in much Victorian writing. Indeed, we have already encountered it in Tennyson's description of death in "Lancelot and Elaine", calling "like a friend's voice from a distant field/Approaching through the darkness". In her very popular 1858 book about churchyards, *God's Acre*, Elizabeth Stone noted that "the much-suffering look on Death not as the destroying angel on the pale horse, not as the ghastly spectre whose unerring dart bears on its point the annihilation of all their joys and pleasures, but as the friend who is to give them release and repose, as the guide who is to lead them home".[8] In a similar spirit, at the very end of the nineteenth century or possibly in the early years of the twentieth, William Henry Draper, the Tractarian vicar of Adel, near Leeds, in his free translation of St Francis of Assisi's "Canticle of the Creatures", *Laudato Si'*, to make the hymn "All creatures of our God and King", rendered the penultimate verse:

> O thou most kind and gentle Death,
> Waiting to hush our latest breath,
> O praise him, Alleluia!
> Thou leadest home the child of God,
> And Christ our Lord the way hath trod.

Draper had lost his first wife shortly after childbirth and a daughter in infancy, and those losses were surely in his mind when he wrote these lines. Later, he was to lose three sons in the First World War.

Adelaide Procter's own experience of the death of her brother at the age of six must similarly have been a factor in the composition of the many poignant poems that she wrote about the death of children. One such, "The Angel's Story", tells of the death of a rich child. An angel arrives, folds him in his arms, spreads his wings and bears him through the air so that "he floats towards the mansions of the blest". This ministering angel turns out to be a poor child who has died:

> Then the radiant angel answered,
> And with holy meaning smiled:
> 'Ere your tender, loving spirit
> Sin and the hard world defiled,
> Mercy gave me leave to seek you;
> I was once that little child.'⁹

She returns again and again in her poems to the theme of deceased children becoming angels. It is expressed particularly powerfully in the deeply sentimental "Links with Heaven", published in her 1862 *Chaplet of Verses*, which is worth quoting in full for its emotional intensity and vivid portrayal of the role of these child angels in heaven:

> OUR God in Heaven, from that holy place,
> To each of us an Angel guide has given;
> But Mothers of dead children have more grace—
> For they give Angels to their God and Heaven.
>
> How can a Mother's heart feel cold or weary
> Knowing her dearer self safe, happy, warm?
> How can she feel her road too dark or dreary
> Who knows her treasure sheltered from the storm?
>
> How can she sin? Our hearts may be unheeding—
> Our God forgot—our holy Saints defied—
> But can a mother hear her dead child pleading
> And thrust those little angel hands aside?
>
> Those little hands stretched down to draw her ever
> Nearer to God by mother love:—we all
> Are blind and weak—yet surely She can never,
> With such a stake in Heaven, fail or fall.

She knows that when the mighty Angels raise
Chorus in Heaven, one little silver tone
is hers for ever—that one little praise,
One little happy voice is all her own.

We may not see her sacred crown of honour,
But all the Angels flitting to and fro
Pause smiling as they pass—they look upon her
As mother of an angel whom they know,

One whom they left nestled at Mary's feet—
The children's place in Heaven—who softly sings
A little chant to please them, slow and sweet,
Or smiling strokes their little folded wings.

Or gives them Her white lilies or Her beads
To play with:—yet, in spite of flower or song
They often lift a wistful look that pleads
And asks Her why their mother stays so long.

Then our dear Queen makes answer she will call
Her very soon: meanwhile they are beguiled
To wait and listen while She tells them all
A story of Her Jesus as a child.

All saints in Heaven may pray with earnest will
And pity for their weak and erring brothers:
Yet there is prayer in Heaven more tender still—
The little Children pleading for their mothers.

Angels of various kinds figure prominently in Adelaide Procter's poems about death and in her envisioning of heaven—indeed it is not too much to say that for her they are its most characteristic and important inhabitants. Alongside the portrayal of deceased children as angels, there are angels whose main role seems to be taking the dead to heaven and others who are messengers telling the living about heaven, as well as the guardian angels who come down from heaven to keep watch over those on earth. Different angelic roles and states are, of course, suggested in Bible passages such as Luke 16:22, which tells of angels carrying the dead beggar to Abraham's side, while the rich man languishes in torment in Hades, and Matthew 22:30 and Luke 20:36 when Jesus says that, at the Resurrection, people will neither marry nor be given in marriage, nor will they die, but rather be like the angels in heaven.

Procter was not the only Victorian devotional poet to populate heaven with angels and point to their various functions. In a verse of his already-quoted hymn "Around the Throne of God a band of glorious Angels ever stand", J. M. Neale distinguishes those angels who stay in heaven constantly praising God from those who come down to earth to guard individuals in this life:

> Some wait around Him, ready still
> To sing His praise and do His will;
> And some, when He commands them, go
> To guard His servants here below.

Christina Rossetti invokes a "passing angel" to give her a taste, or rather a sound bite, of heaven:

> O passing Angel, speed me with a song,
> A melody of heaven to reach my heart
> And rouse me to the race and make me strong;
> Till in such music I take up my part
> Swelling those Hallelujahs full of rest.

No Victorian poet, with the possible exception of John Henry Newman, is quite as keen on angels as Procter, however. Her favourite among the angelic host is the Angel of Death. This seemingly rather forbidding and frightening figure features as a benign and welcoming presence in many of her poems, most famously in the form of "Death's bright angel" in "A Lost Chord", which in Sir Arthur Sullivan's setting was renamed *The Lost Chord*. In this strange poem, which seems to provide a mystical experience of heaven, an organist seeks vainly to strike again the wonderful chord which "linked all perplexed meaning into one perfect peace". He has to conclude that

> it may be that death's bright angel
> Will speak in that chord again;
> It may be that only in Heav'n
> I shall hear that great Amen.

"A Lost Chord" expresses Procter's sense that it is only in heaven that the discordant sounds that fill life here on earth will be brought into harmony. As she puts it in her 1861 poem "Philip and Mildred":

> Heaven unites again the links that Earth has broken!
> For on Earth so much is needed, but in Heaven Love is all!

The Angel of Death has a key role in announcing this unity and harmony that is to be found in heaven and in leading the departed soul towards it. He/she is a hugely positive figure for Procter, as indeed was also the case for the thirteenth-century Persian poet and Sufi mystic Rumi, who wrote that "the angel of death arrives and I spring joyfully up" (and, one might add, for many of those who have had near-death experiences). Her poem "A Chant", based on the Benedictus—many of her poems serve as commentaries to different parts of the Roman Catholic Mass—identifies the different angels who come in the Lord's name as Life, Joy, Pain and Death. The last is in many ways the most important and the one to be most welcomed:

> Who is the Angel that cometh?
> Death!
> But do not shudder and do not fear;

Hold your breath,
For a kingly presence is drawing near,
Cold and bright
Is his flashing steel,
Cold and bright
The smile that comes like a starry light
To calm the terror and grief we feel;
He comes to help and to save and heal:
Then let us, baring our hearts and kneeling
Sing, while we wait this Angel's sword, —
'Blessed is he that cometh
In the name of the Lord!'[10]

Adelaide Procter's best-known poem about the Angel of Death, which was a particular favourite of Queen Victoria, was written in 1858 and in its enthusiastic embrace of death and eager looking forward to the joys and rewards of heaven surely speaks especially powerfully to those, like her, who have endured much physical pain and are finding life increasingly weary and burdensome.

Why shouldst thou fear the beautiful angel, Death,
Who waits thee at the portals of the skies,
Ready to kiss away thy struggling breath,
Ready with gentle hand to close thine eyes?

How many a tranquil soul has passed away,
Fled gladly from fierce pain and pleasures dim,
To the eternal splendour of the day;
And many a troubled heart still calls for him.

Spirits too tender for the battle here
Have turned from life, its hopes, its fears, its charms;
And children, shuddering at a world so drear,
Have smiling passed away into his arms.

> He whom thou fearest will, to ease its pain,
> Lay his cold hand upon thy aching heart:
> Will soothe the terrors of thy troubled brain,
> And bid the shadow of earth's grief depart.
>
> He will give back what neither time, nor might,
> Nor passionate prayer, nor longing hope restore.
> (Dear as to long blind eyes recovered sight,)
> He will give back those who are gone before.
>
> Oh, what were life, if life were all? Thine eyes
> Are blinded by their tears, or thou wouldst see
> Thy treasures wait thee in the far-off skies,
> And Death, thy friend, will give them all to thee.[11]

It is perhaps not surprising that this poem should have been so popular with Victorian readers, the great majority of whom would have experienced the death of a child or close family member or friend. It is immensely reassuring, not least in its promise that in heaven God "will give back those who are gone before", a sure and certain reference to the reuniting of friends and family. At the same time, it acknowledges the genuine fear that accompanies death and the "cold hand" that the Angel of Death lays upon our aching hearts.

For many modern readers, Adelaide Procter's fixation with and positive courting of death will seem unappealingly maudlin and morbid. I fully appreciate that her poems are by no means to everyone's taste, but I ask those who are put off by them to recall the context in which they were written in terms of the short life expectancy and high rates of infant mortality prevailing at the time. Even more than Tennyson's verses, they spring from a deep pastoral concern and compassion as well as from the author's own suffering and sorrow. Perhaps only those who are themselves similarly weary, in pain, and longing for release can really relate to Procter's verses. They certainly speak especially powerfully to those who are in that condition, perhaps none more so than her 1858 poem "A Little Longer", addressed to a beloved friend who is wearying of life and impatient to enter the joys of heaven, portrayed here in theocentric more than anthropocentric terms as a place "where winged Archangels worship,/And trembling bow before the Great White Throne".[12] What this poem conveys above all is Procter's conviction that it is in heaven that we find our true, immortal life, of which this life is but a mere shadow. Like Tennyson, although even more explicitly and emphatically, both her belief that there is a heaven, and her understanding of what it is like, are grounded on her faith in God's love, that "Love divine" in harmony with which our human hearts will beat for ever and the angel voices "shall ring in heavenly chant".

> A little longer still—Patience, Belovèd:
> A little longer still, ere Heaven unroll
> The Glory, and the Brightness, and the wonder,
> Eternal, and divine, that waits thy Soul!
>
> A little longer ere Life true, immortal,
> (Not this our shadowy Life,) will be thine own;
> And thou shalt stand where winged Archangels worship,
> And trembling bow before the Great White Throne.
>
> A little longer still, and Heaven awaits thee,
> And fills thy spirit with a great delight;
> Then our pale joys will seem a dream forgotten,
> Our Sun a darkness, and our Day a Night.
>
> A little longer, and thy Heart, Belovèd,
> Shall beat for ever with a Love divine;
> And joy so pure, so mighty, so eternal,
> No creature knows and lives, will then be thine.
>
> A little longer yet—and angel voices
> Shall ring in heavenly chant upon thine ear;
> Angels and Saints await thee, and God needs thee:
> Beloved, can we bid thee linger here![13]

## Notes

1 Adelaide Anne Procter, *A Chaplet of Verses* (London: Longmans, Green, 1862), p. 65.
2 Adelaide Anne Procter, *The Poems* (Boston: Ticknor & Fields, 1864), p. 45.
3 Adelaide Anne Procter, *Legends and Lyrics* (London: George Bell, 1888), pp. xxi–ii.
4 Ferdinand Janku, *Adelaide Anne Procter: Ihr Leben und ihre Werke* (Wien: Wilhelm Braumüller, 1912), p. 89.
5 Gill Gregory, *The Life and Work of Adelaide Procter* (Aldershot: Ashgate, 1998), p. 14. On this, see also Chapter 6 of Karen Dieleman, *Religious Imaginaries: The Liturgical and Poetic Practices of Elizabeth Barrett Browning, Christina Rossetti and Adelaide Procter* (Athens, OH: Ohio University Press, 2012).
6 Procter, *Legends and Lyrics*, p. 342.
7 Procter, *Legends and Lyrics*, pp. 121–2.
8 Elizabeth Stone, *God's Acre: Historical Notices Relating to Churchyards* (London: John W. Parker, 1858), p. 31.
9 Procter, *Legends and Lyrics*, p. 8.
10 Adelaide Anne Procter, *The Poems* (Boston: Ticknor & Fields, 1864), p. 413.
11 Procter, *Legends and Lyrics*, p. 255.
12 Procter, *Legends and Lyrics*, p. 73.
13 Procter, *Legends and Lyrics*, pp. 149–50.

# 4
# "It's oh in Paradise that I fain would be"

*Christina Rossetti*

Christina Rossetti (1830–94), remembered today chiefly as the author of "In the Bleak Midwinter", was the leading devotional poet of the Victorian age. Of Anglo-Italian extraction, she grew up in the Church of England and was deeply influenced by the Tractarian movement. While she remained a devout High Anglican throughout her life, she was not without religious doubts and fears.

Periodic bouts of severe depression and ill health encouraged a certain introspective tendency, and she poured much of herself into her poetry. In his entry on her in the 1911 *Encyclopaedia Britannica*, fellow poet Edmund Gosse wrote: "Hers was a cloistered spirit, timid, nun-like, bowed down by suffering and humility; her character was so retiring as to be almost invisible. All that we really need to know about her, save that she was a great saint, was that she was a great poet."[1] She is often bracketed with Adelaide Procter as a sickly and frustrated Victorian spinster with an unusually morbid obsession. This is unjust and inaccurate in respect of both women. Christina Rossetti took an active interest in politics, in the artistic endeavours of the Pre-Raphaelite Brotherhood, of which her brother Gabriel was a leading member, and in the running of Highgate Penitentiary, a refuge for fallen women, where she was a regular volunteer helper.

It is certainly true that she wrote a great deal about death and what follows it. Her biographer Marya Zaturenska describes her first and foremost as "the poet of death, the poet of the death-wish".[2] Her fixation on this topic can partly be explained by the serious illness which afflicted her from childhood and recurred throughout her life, her strict religious upbringing in which Anglo-Catholic doctrines and influences were to the fore, and her strong and perhaps overactive imagination. She was also profoundly touched by the deaths of those close to her, including her sister Maria, an Anglican nun, at the age of 49, her brother Gabriel at 54, her infant nephew Michael, and Charles Cayley, a fellow poet and translator to whom she had been deeply attached, at the age of 60. Their deaths, and the loss of her parents, reinforced her sense of the impermanence of relationships and values in this world and her yearning for the enduring love which she hoped would be found in the next one.

Although Christina Rossetti had a clear sense of the reality of divine judgment, the separation of the sheep and goats and the fact that not everyone would go to heaven, she never wrote about hell. That did not mean that she was without fear of it. Her older brother William noted that, largely as a result of her youthful exposure to some of the more severe doctrines of the Oxford Movement, she acquired "an awful sense of unworthiness, shadowed by an awful certainty of the reality of hell".[3] The emphasis throughout her poetry, however, is almost entirely on heaven, and although she accepts that it is not certain that she will go there, and there is the occasional wobble in her writing about whether she will make it, the overall theme is a clearly expressed hope that it is her destination, coupled at times with a longing and yearning similar to that of Adelaide Procter. She does also periodically express her profound fear of death and its darkness. Although she absolutely foreswore the spiritualism that gripped many of her contemporaries, she had frequent nightmares, expressed in some of her poems, about the unquiet dead, ghosts and wandering spirits drifting around.

In many ways, her view of heaven was simple, traditional and biblical, and very similar to that expressed in the popular children's hymns of the time, as discussed in Chapter 1. This comes across in the second poem she ever wrote, which was composed at the age of 11:

> What is heaven? 'tis a country
> Far away from mortal ken;
> 'Tis a land, where by God's bounty,
> After death live righteous men.

> That that blest land I may enter,
> Is my humble, earnest cry;
> Lord! Admit me to Thy presence,
> Lord, admit me, or I die.[4]

She did not really deviate much from this view throughout her life, continuing to see heaven as another, far-off country, a place of rest, where in the words of her poem "Up-Hill" there will be "beds for all who come" and where friends and family will meet again. Indeed, she takes this last idea further and suggests that love affairs which have begun but been broken off on earth will be completed and consummated in heaven. At the end of her poem "The Convent Threshold", a young girl addresses the lover she is rejecting to become a nun and, speaking of heaven, tells him, "There we shall meet as once we met and love with old familiar love." Perhaps she was influenced here by the teaching of her great mentor, the pioneer Tractarian Edward Pusey, who wrote to Charles Dodgson, the father of the author with the same name better known as Lewis Carroll, when he was mourning the death of his wife:

> I have often thought, since I had to think of this, how, in all adversity, what God takes away He may give us back with increase. One cannot think that any holy earthly love will cease, when we shall 'be like the Angels of God in Heaven'. Love here must shadow our love there, deeper because spiritual, without any alloy from our sinful nature, and in the fulness of the love of God. But as we grow here by God's grace will be our capacity for endless love.[5]

In her *Literary Biography*, Jan Marsh sees a progression in Christina Rossetti's thought about heaven: "At first a paradisal dream land, where all sorrows and disappointments would fade into insignificance, heaven became an Ideal realm, dimly apprehended in life but representing the ultimate reality."[6] I am not sure that there is as much of a transition as Marsh suggests, but it is certainly true that there is a very strong Platonic strain to Rossetti's thinking about the relationship between the earthly and the divine, which she conceives of as that between the imperfect and perfect, the actual and ideal. This world is but a shadowland. Heaven is the real world, and it is marked above all by the love that is found on earth but always imperfectly and impermanently. Rossetti does not dwell on the sorrows and failings of life in this world in the way that Procter does. Indeed, she is very affirmative of its joys and positive qualities. What she emphatically does believe, however, is that heaven will be even better and that in this life we get only partial and occasional glimpses of its wonders.

This conviction that heaven will be like earth, only better because it will be without earth's imperfections, is expressed in another early poem, "Earth and Heaven", written when she had just turned 14. It begins with a catalogue of the wonders and beauties of the earth, from "the water calmly flowing" and "the sweet rose that blushes" to the skylark's soaring motion. It then poses the question as to whether "our promised Heaven" really will yield any greater charms than this and answers it roundly in the affirmative:

> Yes; For aye in Heav'n doth dwell
> Glowing, indestructible,
> What here below finds tainted birth
> In the corrupted sons of Earth;
> For, filling there and satisfying
> Man's soul unchanging and undying,
> Earth's fleeting joys and beauties far above,
> In Heaven is Love.[7]

Alongside this idea that heaven is filled and suffused with love in a way that earth is not, Rossetti also strongly expresses the biblical concept of a new creation whereby the earth is not ultimately destroyed or swallowed up by heaven but rather completed and perfected in a new divine dispensation informed by harmony and love. Taking seriously the teaching found in the Book of Revelation of a new heaven and a new earth, she looks forward to the restoration of the prelapsarian world of the Garden of Eden before sin and evil stalked the earth. The connection between the primal prelapsarian state and the consummation which is to come is explored in her poem "Sexagesima", first published in 1892 as part of a devotional commentary on the Apocalypse:

> Yet Earth was very good in days of old,
> And Earth is lovely still:
> Still for the sacred flock she spreads the fold,
> For Sion rears the hill.
>
> Mother she is, and cradle of our race,
> A depth where treasures lie,
> The broad foundation of a holy place,
> Man's step to scale the sky.
>
> She spreads the harvest-field which Angels reap,
> And lo! the crop is white;
> She spreads God's Acre where the happy sleep
> All night that is not night.
>
> Earth may not pass till Heaven shall pass away,
> Nor Heaven may be renewed
> Except with Earth: and once more in that day
> Earth shall be very good.[8]

The last verse of that poem brings to mind the line "Heaven and earth shall flee away when He comes to reign" in "In the Bleak Midwinter". Rossetti does not shun the difficult doctrine of Christ's second coming and the impact that it will have on heaven and earth. Both will be swept away in their present form, and both renewed. The second coming will usher in a new marriage of earth and heaven where the former will not be abandoned or destroyed but rebuilt in a purer, more splendid form with the recovery of the innocence that existed before the fall, but with something more added in terms of the fulfilment of God's plan and the reign of transcendent love.

    The implications of this new heaven and earth are never quite worked out in terms of our ultimate human destination: are we, in fact, destined to live eternally in the new earth rather than the new heaven or are they somehow one and the same or contiguous? For the most part, Rossetti seems to remain more focused on heaven, albeit the new heaven, and to see our destiny as being to dwell there eternally, enjoying all that we have enjoyed on earth and more. This comes over in her 1854 poem "Paradise", which sticks very closely to the picture given in the Book of Revelation:

> Once in a dream I saw the flowers
> That bud and bloom in Paradise;
> More fair they are than waking eyes
> Have seen in all this world of ours.
> And faint the perfume-bearing rose,
> And faint the lily on its stem,
> And faint the perfect violet
> Compared with them.
>
> I heard the songs of Paradise:
> Each bird sat singing in his place;
> A tender song so full of grace
> It soared like incense to the skies.
> Each bird sat singing to his mate
> Soft cooing notes among the trees:
> The nightingale herself were cold
> To such as these.
>
> I saw the fourfold River flow,
> And deep it was, with golden sand;
> It flowed between a mossy land
> With murmured music grave and low.
> It hath refreshment for all thirst,
> For fainting spirits strength and rest:
> Earth holds not such a draught as this
> From east to west.

> The Tree of Life stood budding there,
> Abundant with its twelvefold fruits;
> Eternal sap sustains its roots,
> Its shadowing branches fill the air.
> Its leaves are healing for the world,
> Its fruit the hungry world can feed,
> Sweeter than honey to the taste
> And balm indeed.
>
> I saw the gate called Beautiful;
> And looked, but scarce could look, within;
> I saw the golden streets begin,
> And outskirts of the glassy pool.
> Oh harps, oh crowns of plenteous stars,
> Oh green palm-branches many-leaved—
> Eye hath not seen, nor ear hath heard,
> Nor heart conceived.
>
> I hope to see these things again,
> But not as once in dreams by night;
> To see them with my very sight,
> And touch, and handle, and attain:
> To have all Heaven beneath my feet
> For narrow way that once they trod;
> To have my part with all the saints,
> And with my God.[9]

It is significant that this vision of the next world is conceived as a dream. Many of Christina Rossetti's poems about heaven are expressed in similar terms. There is sometimes a hint of worry that heaven is just a dream and a state that exists in the mind rather than as an objective reality. But although this thought does occasionally trouble her, for the most part she writes in the belief and hope that it is a real place, the ultimate abode of all those loved by God. At times, she expresses a yearning and longing for it reminiscent of that found much more frequently in Adelaide Procter's verses, as in her 1875 poem "Saints and Angels", which seems to confirm Marya Zaturenska's description of her as "the poet of the death-wish":

> It's oh in Paradise that I fain would be,
> Away from earth and weariness and all beside;
> Earth is too full of loss with its dividing sea,
> But Paradise upbuilds the bower for the bride.
>
> Where flowers are yet in bud while the boughs are green,
> I would get quit of earth and get robed for heaven;
> Putting on my raiment white within the screen,
> Putting on my crown of gold whose gems are seven.
>
> This life is but the passage of a day,
> This life is but a pang and all is over;
> But in the life to come which fades not away
> Every love shall abide and every lover.[10]

There are several more original themes in Rossetti's treatment of the afterlife. Perhaps the most striking is the way that she deals with the state of souls after death if they do not go straight to heaven as a doctrine of immortality would suggest, but rather have to wait for the second coming of Christ, the last judgment and the general resurrection at the end of time as suggested by more orthodox Christian teaching. Rossetti tackles this difficult question by invoking the idea of the "soul sleep", a long period of suspended animation after death in which souls rest in limbo. Characteristically, she uses the analogy of dreaming to describe this state in which the souls of the dead dream of Paradise while not yet fully enjoying it. Many of her poems dwell on this state of "soul sleep". One of the earliest, written when she was 18, captures its dreamlike state where there is a suspension of feeling and a kind of ambivalence between remembering and forgetting, but no cause for sadness or mourning among those left behind:

> When I am dead, my dearest,
> Sing no sad songs for me;
> Plant thou no roses at my head,
> Nor shady cypress tree:
> Be the green grass above me
> With showers and dewdrops wet;
> And if thou wilt, remember,
> And if thou wilt, forget.
>
> I shall not see the shadows,
> I shall not feel the rain;
> I shall not hear the nightingale
> Sing on, as if in pain:
> And dreaming through the twilight
> That doth not rise nor set,
> Haply I may remember,
> And haply may forget.[11]

A poem written a year later, when she was 19, entitled "Dream Land", describes a female in a state of soul sleep. This "charmed sleep" becomes deeper and deeper and is not to be woken from. The references to her face being "toward the west" and to "sleep that no pain shall wake" suggest that the subject of the poem is indeed experiencing the sleep-like rest from the toils and travails of life that comes with death, as described in Hamlet's famous soliloquy: "To die: to sleep . . . and by a sleep to say we end the heart-ache and the thousand natural shocks that flesh is heir to":

> Where sunless rivers weep
> Their waves into the deep,
> She sleeps a charmed sleep:
> Awake her not.
> Led by a single star,
> She came from very far
> To seek where shadows are
> Her pleasant lot.

She left the rosy morn,
She left the fields of corn,
For twilight cold and lorn
And water springs.
Through sleep, as through a veil,
She sees the sky look pale,
And hears the nightingale
That sadly sings.

Rest, rest, a perfect rest
Shed over brow and breast;
Her face is toward the west,
The purple land.
She cannot see the grain
Ripening on hill and plain;
She cannot feel the rain
Upon her hand.

Rest, rest, for evermore
Upon a mossy shore;
Rest, rest at the heart's core
Till time shall cease:
Sleep that no pain shall wake;
Night that no morn shall break
Till joy shall overtake
Her perfect peace.[12]

Coloured illustrations made by the author to accompany this poem show a somewhat sepulchral-looking figure clad in white and holding a cross leaving behind the steep slope of a purple hill and ascending in winged form.

Another poem, written in the same year as "Dream Land" (1849) and entitled "Rest", embellishes the theme of soul sleep as the lengthy initial stage of death by invoking the rather chilling and stifling image of the earth which is pressing down on the coffin of another dead female, sealing her sweet eyes and leaving no room for mirth. Yet it is also providing a kind of cocoon, "hushed in and curtained" against all that had troubled and irked her in this life. Darkness and stillness characterize the lengthy sleep that awaits us until the judgment day, but it is not to be feared—its silence is more musical than any song, its rest is eternal and when the soul does eventually wake on the morning of eternity it will not seem as though the period of waiting has been long:

> O Earth, lie heavily upon her eyes;
> Seal her sweet eyes weary of watching, Earth;
> Lie close around her; leave no room for mirth
> With its harsh laughter, nor for sound of sighs.
> She hath no questions, she hath no replies,
> Hushed in and curtained with a blessed dearth
> Of all that irked her from the hour of birth;
> With stillness that is almost Paradise.
> Darkness more clear than noonday holdeth her,
> Silence more musical than any song;
> Even her very heart has ceased to stir:
> Until the morning of Eternity
> Her rest shall not begin nor end, but be;
> And when she wakes she will not think it long.[13]

A third poem dating from 1849, entitled "Life Hidden" and written like "Rest" in sonnet form, makes an even more explicit evocation of the long sleep of death, which is here presented as an ambiguous state where there is no dreaming, feeling or hearing yet still a sensibility, a capacity to count the flight of time and an overarching, prevailing sense of peace:

> Roses and lilies grow above the place
> Where she sleeps the long sleep that doth not dream.
> If we could look upon her hidden face
> Nor shadow would be there nor garish gleam
> Of light: her life is lapsing like a stream
> That makes no noise but floweth on apace
> Seawards; while many a shade and shady beam
> Vary the ripples in their gliding chase.
> She doth not see, but knows: she doth not feel,
> And yet is sensible: she hears no sound,
> Yet counts the flight of time and doth not err.
> Peace far and near; peace to ourselves and her:
> Her body is at peace in holy ground,
> Her spirit is at peace where Angels kneel.[14]

The likening of death to a river running into the sea, expressed in the line in the poem above, "her life is lapsing like a stream that makes no noise but floweth on apace seawards", is a popular theme in Christina Rossetti's poetry. It occurs again in "An Immurata Sister":

> Life flows down to death; we cannot bind
> That current that it should not flee:
> Life flows down to death, as rivers find
> The inevitable sea.[15]

The last line of that extract employs the same phrase, "the inevitable sea", that Arthur Hugh Clough uses in his 1858 poem "O stream, descending to the sea" (p. 157). The fullest expression of this particular metaphor for death is found in "Christ is our All in All", part of a devotional meditation on the Book of Revelation entitled "The Face of the Deep" that Christina Rossetti wrote shortly before her own death in 1892. It conveys a wonderful sense of our individual waters mingling with those of God's shoreless sea:

> Lord, we are rivers running to Thy sea,
> Our waves and ripples all derived from Thee:
> A nothing we should have, a nothing be,
> Except for Thee.
>
> Sweet are the waters of Thy shoreless sea,
> Make sweet our waters that make haste to Thee;
> Pour in Thy sweetness, that ourselves may be
> Sweetness to Thee.[16]

At times, she expresses a frustration that heaven seems so distant and far off. Her poem "De Profundis" begins:

> Oh why is heaven built so far,
> Oh why is earth set so remote?
> I cannot reach the nearest star
> That hangs afloat.

It ends with an expression of unworthiness and uncertainty and a distinctly Tennysonian note of stretching lame hands of faith and faintly trusting the larger hope:

> For I am bound with fleshly bands,
> Joy, beauty, lie beyond my scope;
> I strain my heart, I stretch my hands
> And catch at hope.[17]

If Rossetti sometimes finds heaven just too remote and unattainable, and even if she occasionally falls prey to doubts about its very existence, she also has a clear sense that to some extent it is to be found here and now within ourselves. Jan Marsh comments that "in her figuration, heaven remained an eternal promise but also a concept of everyday aspiration. We have to lay its deep foundations through our own lives and faith".[18] A poem written in 1854 extols the role of faith and hope in creating heaven's boundary wall and secret bower and somehow suggests that it is nearer than we might think:

Our heaven must be within ourselves,
Our home and heaven the work of faith
All thro' this race of life which shelves
Downward to death.

So faith shall build the boundary wall,
And hope shall plant the secret bower,
That both may show magnifical
With gem and flower.

While over all a dome must spread,
And love shall be that dome above;
And deep foundations must be laid,
And these are love.[19]

Alongside her original and extensive exploration of "soul sleep", Christina Rossetti made another distinctive contribution to Victorian thinking about death through her reflections on its positive physical and organic consequences, with decaying human remains providing the compost out of which new life will grow. She herself was something of a pioneer environmentalist, expressing a strong desire to be buried in a biodegradable wicker coffin so that her body could disintegrate into the earth and fertilize it. The strong ecological strain in her thought and writing is emphasized by her latest biographer, Emma Mason.[20] Her sense that the process of recycling in nature literally brought life out of death and thus created its own afterlife and continuing existence was shared by several other mid-nineteenth-century poets, notably John Clare in "All nature has a feeling" (1845) and Walt Whitman in "This Compost" (1856) (quoted on pp. 142–3). It was part of a wider Victorian understanding of the naturalness and the value of death in terms of creating the conditions for new life which is explored further in Chapter 9.

In Rossetti's poems, reflections about this positive aspect of death are often expressed as the thoughts of someone walking through a graveyard. As we have already noted, the nineteenth century saw a huge expansion of graveyards and cemeteries, described reverentially as "God's Acres", and often carefully tended with flowers growing over the graves. Rossetti excels in the genre of "graveyard poems" which first developed in the eighteenth century. Her 1849 poem "Sweet Death" is one of the finest, lacking the rather macabre character of so many children's hymns on the subject and rather presenting a vision of a unified divine reality that has no end. Walking daily through a churchyard on her way to pray, the author is struck by the way that the sweetest flowers on the graves die and fall "to nourish the rich earth". So it is with humans: young and beautiful people die like flowers, their bodies returning to the earth and their souls going to heaven. This leads to a reflection on how life is sweet, but death is sweeter, turning all colours to green, and on how the permanence and truth of God surpass worldly preoccupations like youth and beauty. The "full harvest" of death is preferable to the meagre yield of earthly crops as represented by Ruth's gleanings of what was left over at the edge of fields described in the Old Testament.

> The sweetest blossoms die.
> And so it was that, going day by day
> Unto the church to praise and pray,
> And crossing the green churchyard thoughtfully,
> I saw how on the graves the flowers
> Shed their fresh leaves in showers,
> And how their perfume rose up to the sky
> Before it passed away.
>
> The youngest blossoms die.
> They die, and fall and nourish the rich earth
> From which they lately had their birth;
> Sweet life, but sweeter death that passeth by
> And is as though it had not been:—
> All colours turn to green:
> The bright hues vanish, and the odours fly,
> The grass hath lasting worth.

> And youth and beauty die.
> So be it, O my God, Thou God of truth:
> Better than beauty and than youth
> Are Saints and Angels, a glad company;
> And Thou, O Lord, our Rest and Ease,
> Are better far than these.
> Why should we shrink from our full harvest? why
> Prefer to glean with Ruth?[21]

This last image is recalled in Edith Sitwell's poem "Eurydice" in the lines "Love is not changed by Death, and nothing is lost and all in the end is harvest". Rossetti returns to a graveyard setting in her 1855 poem "I have a message unto thee", which she notes was "written in sickness". In it, she writes about young brides wearing flowers, going on to reflect "but next we plant them in garden plots of death" and finally answering clearly the question she poses as to "Whose lot is best":

> Dear are the blossoms
> For bride or maiden's head,
> But dearer planted
> Around our blessed dead.
> Those mind us of decay
> And joys that fade away,
> These preach to us perfection,
> Long love and resurrection.
> We make our graveyards fair,
> For spirit-like birds of air,
> For Angels may be finding there
> Lost Eden's own delection.[22]

Here once again is Rossetti's sense of heaven as the recreation of the Lost Eden, anticipated here on earth in graveyards over which hover angels and spirit-like birds of air. There is a hint, too, of her view that the new creation will be one in which humans live harmoniously with the rest of the animal and natural world. Heaven, or perhaps more accurately the new heaven and earth, will indeed be a place where the lion will lie down with the lamb and they will not hurt or destroy in all God's holy mountain. She writes several poems about the natural wonders that are to be found in heaven—a striking one from 1864 describes "The Birds of Paradise"—and the way in which they will reflect the full pleroma of God's creation, with humans in their rightful place and not dominating every other species.

Critics and cynics might say that there is too much wishful thinking and pie-in-the-sky sentimentalism in Christina Rossetti's poems about heaven. They are the product of a vivid poetic imagination and a deep Christian faith. Although many of those that I have quoted in this chapter come from her teenage years, she remained fixated on the subject until the end of her life. The poem that was, according to a note scribbled by her brother William on the back of the manuscript, "the last that C ever wrote—perhaps late in 1893 or early in 94", draws together several of the most recurrent themes in her writing about heaven—the yearning and longing for it, the sense of its almost physical location overarching land and sea, the contrast with "earth-sadness", the reliance on biblical language and imagery ("no more sea", an image that rather conflicts with her description of our waters mingling with those of God's "shoreless sea") and the way it is mirrored and anticipated in gardens and graveyards:

> Heaven overarches earth and sea,
> Earth-sadness and sea-bitterness;
> Heaven overarches you and me:
> A little while, and we shall be
> (Please God) where there is no more sea
> Or barren wilderness.
>
> Heaven overarches you and me
> And all earth's gardens and her graves:
> Look up with me, until we see
> The day break and the shadows flee;
> What tho' tonight wrecks you and me,
> If so tomorrow saves?[23]

## Notes

1. *Encyclopaedia Britannica*, 11th edn, Vol. 23 (Cambridge: Cambridge University Press, 1911), p. 747.
2. Marya Zaturenska, *Christina Rossetti: A Portrait with Background* (New York: Macmillan, 1949), p. 229.
3. Jan Marsh, *Christina Rossetti: A Literary Biography* (London: Jonathan Cape, 1994), p. 64.
4. Christina Rossetti, *The Complete Poems* (Harmondsworth: Penguin, 2001), p. 649.
5. Stuart Dodgson Collingwood, *The Life and Letters of Lewis Carroll* (New York: The Century Co., 1899), pp. 48–9.
6. Marsh, *Christina Rossetti*, p. 342.
7. Rossetti, *Complete Poems*, p. 618.
8. Rossetti, *Complete Poems*, pp. 427–8.
9. Rossetti, *Complete Poems*, p. 215.
10. Rossetti, *Complete Poems*, p. 223.
11. Rossetti, *Complete Poems*, p. 52.
12. Rossetti, *Complete Poems*, p. 21.
13. Rossetti, *Complete Poems*, pp. 54–5.
14. Rossetti, *Complete Poems*, pp. 709–10.
15. Rossetti, *Complete Poems*, p. 328.
16. Rossetti, *Complete Poems*, p. 397.
17. Rossetti, *Complete Poems*, p. 302.
18. Marsh, *Christina Rossetti*, p. 342.
19. Rossetti, *Complete Poems*, p. 523.
20. Emma Mason, *Christina Rossetti: Poetry, Ecology, Faith* (Oxford: Oxford University Press, 2018).
21. Rossetti, *Complete Poems*, pp. 68–9.
22. Rossetti, *Complete Poems*, p. 771.
23. Rossetti, *Complete Poems*, p. 87.

5

# "We know them living unto Thee"

*John Ellerton*

John Ellerton (1826–93) is best remembered for his evening hymn, "The day Thou gavest, Lord, is ended", which still often features in lists of the top ten favourite British hymns and continues to be much used at funeral and memorial services. Altogether, he wrote more than 80 hymns, including several specifically for use at funerals, notably "Now the labourer's task is o'er" and "God of the living in whose eyes". Like "The day Thou gavest", they are infused not just with rich poetic imagery and a sense of calm reassurance but also, and arguably more valuably, with a deep pastoral intent and sensitivity.

Ellerton spent his life as a parish priest and this experience is at the root of the gentle pastoral approach shown in his hymns. Indeed, in many ways he stands as the archetypal Victorian vicar, learned and literary while also being deeply committed to both the physical and spiritual needs of his parishioners. He grew up in the Lake District and was educated at King William's College on the Isle of Man and Trinity College, Cambridge. As an undergraduate, he was deeply influenced by the writings of F. D. Maurice, whose liberal Broad Church sympathies he came to espouse. He was also influenced by Maurice's Christian socialism and by the writings of Charles Kingsley and Arthur Clough.

After serving curacies in Sussex at Easebourne and Brighton, where he set up a night school for working men, he went in 1860 as the first vicar of St Michael and All Angels church in Crewe Green, Staffordshire. He was deeply involved in the Mechanics Institute, which was set up for the educational needs of the large number of workers in the railway locomotive works there. In 1872, he moved to Shropshire as rector of Hinstock and in 1876 became rector of Barnes in southwest London.

Following a breakdown in his health, he moved in 1885 to his final parish, White Roding in Essex.

In several respects, Ellerton's funeral hymns and his approach to death and heaven conform to the prevailing tone of Victorian hymnody as explored in Chapter 1. An evening hymn which he wrote for children, "The hours of day are over", looks forward to "the home prepared by Jesus for us above the sky" and concludes:

> Lord, gather all Thy children
> To meet Thee there at last,
> When earthly tasks are ended,
> And earthly days are past;
> With all our dear ones round us
> In that eternal home,
> Where death no more shall part us,
> And night shall never come.

Another hymn, "When the day of toil is done", was first sung in 1870 at the funeral of the chief manager of the Crewe railway works, who had died at the age of 35. Specially written for the service, it makes much of the theme of everlasting rest and ends with a simple and reassuring affirmation of the hope of eternal life:

> When the breath of life is flown,
> When the grave must claim its own,
> Lord of life, be ours Thy crown,—
> Life for evermore.

"God of the living", Ellerton's greatest and most controversial hymn about death and what follows it, was originally written for use at the funerals of children. He wrote it while at Brighton, where he was often called on to take funerals of those who had died in infancy and childhood, for a book of *Hymns for School and Bible Classes*, which he edited for publication in 1859. This original children's version runs as follows:

God of the living, to whose eye
All worlds Thou madest open lie;
All souls are Thine; we must not say
That those are dead we mourn today;
From this vain world of flesh set free;
We know them living unto thee.

They are not dead, for Thou art just:
To Thee we leave them, Lord, in trust;
And bless Thee for the love which gave
Thy Son to fill a human grave,
That none might dread that realm unknown,
Or fear to go where Christ has gone.

Still do we love them as of old,
Still count them kept in Jesus' fold,
Still do we share their faith and joy,
Still join our voice in their employ,
and Thee in them, O Lord most high,
and them in Thee, we magnify.

There are several striking features in this hymn. The second verse has that telling reference to God in his love sending Jesus to "fill a human grave" and in this way taking away our dread of what follows death. The third verse powerfully conveys the idea that the living continue to be united with the dead, sharing their faith and joy and joining "our voice in their employ". This last image recalls Charles Wesley's belief that we are closest to the communion of saints when singing hymns and echoes the line in Edward Bickersteth's hymn, "For my sake and the Gospel's, go and tell redemption's story", which proclaims that "in concert with the holy dead the warrior church rejoices". But the most dramatic and original feature in Ellerton's hymn is its emphatic assertion that those we mourn are not in fact dead because they are living unto God.

Ellerton revised "God of the living" in 1867 while he was at Crewe Green for use in the funerals of those who were not regular churchgoers. This new version, which was published in several hymn books, notably in *Church Hymns* (1871) of which he was a co-editor along with William Walsham How and Robert Brown-Borthwick, goes as follows:

> God of the living, in whose eyes
> Unveiled Thy whole creation lies,
> All souls are Thine, we must not say
> That those are dead who pass away;
> From this our world of flesh set free,
> We know them living unto Thee.
>
> Released from earthly toil and strife,
> With Thee is hidden still their life;
> Thine are their thoughts, their works, their powers,
> All Thine, and yet most truly ours;
> For well we know, where'er they be,
> Our dead are living unto Thee.
>
> Not spilt like water on the ground,
> Not wrapped in dreamless sleep profound,
> Not wandering in unknown despair,
> Beyond Thy voice, Thine Arm, Thy care;
> Not left to lie like fallen tree—
> Not dead, but living, unto Thee.
>
> Thy Word is true, Thy will is just;
> To Thee we leave them, Lord, in trust;
> And bless Thee for the love which gave
> Thy Son to fill a human grave;
> That none might fear that world to see
> Where all are living unto Thee.

> O Breather into man of breath,
> O Holder of the keys of death,
> O Giver of the life within,
> Save us from death, the death of sin,
> That body, soul, and spirit be
> Forever living unto Thee.

This revised version of the hymn asserts even more emphatically than in the original children's version that, far from being dead, those who have passed from this life are living unto God, by whom their thoughts, words and powers are held and preserved. It also seems to convey a strong suggestion that the dead go straight to heaven and are not "wrapped in dreamless sleep", nor "wandering in unknown despair". There is also a distinct universalist message in the phrase in the first verse "all souls are thine", confirmed in the statement in the fourth verse that Jesus' death means that "none might fear that world to see/Where all are living unto Thee". These aspects of the hymn caused considerable unease to the editors of *Hymns Ancient & Modern*, who were unhappy about its universalist implications and its apparent denial of the doctrines of hell, judgment and conditional atonement. They were not prepared to include it in the first (1868) appendix to the hymnal unless it was substantially altered. Ellerton refused to change it and sent the proprietors this staunch defence of his hymn:

> Its object is to put forward the Christian view of death, not as regards those only of whom we can cherish the *sure and certain hope* of rest in Christ, but as regards all those over whom we are called to say the Burial Service, and therefore in whose case we are likely to require an appropriate hymn. I do not wish to deny that the unbelievers who *pass away* are indeed *dead*; But then they were *dead while they lived*; I wish to lay stress on the fact that our Lord does not call the mere dissolution of the body by the name of death; That the soul is still living, not beyond the reach, if God wills, of His infinite mercy. Surely I say no more than the Fathers imply again and again.

I do *not deny* Hell, or *assert* Purgatory; I merely say that the soul which departs from the body does not depart from the range of God's love. Surely it is recalling the worst side of doctrinal Calvinism to assert this only of those few whom we can honestly call faithful Christians. The belief that *all live with Him* is the only belief which can justify the Church in expressing hope in the Burial Service over all whatsoever their lives who are not formally excommunicate. Most of our funeral hymns either presuppose that the deceased was an eminent saint, or else say nothing which can give definite hope and comfort to mourners at the very moment when their hearts are most ready to receive the Gospel of God's love.

I do not put forward my hymn as one of any special merit; but such as it is, it has a definite meaning. If I were to write one applicable only to those who die with clear evidences of a state of grace, I should only do badly what hundreds have done well. If then you think it wise, in deference to the Protestant mind, to withdraw all suggestion of a possibility of mercy in the future life for the great mass of our parishioners, it would be I think better for you to cancel the hymn. I am afraid I cannot alter it without destroying it.[1]

In the event, the editors of *Hymns Ancient & Modern* did not include "God of the living" in the 1868 appendix. It did appear in the 1889 supplement but was dropped again from the 1904 edition. Other hymn book editors were less worried and saw its pastoral worth, and it appeared in over 50 hymnals in the later nineteenth and early twentieth centuries. I myself lobbied successfully for its inclusion in the current (fourth) edition of the Church of Scotland's *Church Hymnary*.

John Ellerton's lengthy apologia makes clear that this hymn was born out of his own pastoral experience in taking parish funerals of those who were not churchgoers and who were, as most of us are, neither shining saints nor spectacular sinners. It is surely one of the most affirmative and appealing Victorian statements about life after death, beautifully expressed and profoundly consoling for the grieving. I have it on the list of hymns for my own funeral, to be sung to John Bacchus Dykes' tune

MELITA, which fits it perfectly. Its repeated message that the dead are not spilt like water on the ground or left to lie like fallen trees, but rather live on in God's mind and love ("Thine are their thoughts, their works, their powers"), suggests that what is most distinctive about the whole human person is preserved in God. This seems to me to be somewhat similar to the view held by the theoretical physicist and Anglican priest John Polkinghorne, that God holds us all in his divine memory, somewhat like a computer server. As he put it:

> In natural terms the pattern that is me, whatever form it actually takes, will be dissolved at my death, as my body decays and my relationships are reduced simply to the fading retention of memories by others. Yet it seems an entirely coherent belief that the everlastingly faithful God will hold that pattern perfectly preserved in the divine memory, and then embody it in the ultimate divine eschatological act of resurrection at the last day, as the new creation enters into the unfolding fullness of time.[2]

There are also echoes of Ellerton's thought in the theory of "objective immortality" put forward by process theologians, notably the twentieth-century American philosopher Charles Hartshorne. For him, our life is like a book, of which birth is the first page and death the last. The reader of this book is God, in whose mind or memory it is everlastingly preserved and can be used in the ongoing work of creation. "Our adequate immortality can only be God's omniscience of us," Hartshorne writes. "He to whom all hearts are open remains evermore open to any heart that has ever been apparent to Him. We live on, not so much as thinking, acting, feeling, responding subjects but objectively in the mind and memory of God."[3]

Despite his observation in "God of the living" that the dead are "not wrapped in dreamless sleep profound", Ellerton did subscribe to the orthodox Christian view that the post-mortem state is one of sleep until the general resurrection of the dead and not an immediate ascent to heaven. This is confirmed by what he wrote about this verse in Christopher Wordsworth's hymn "Hark, the sound of holy voices, chanting at the crystal sea", which was omitted from the first edition of *Church Hymns* because of its apparent departure from this doctrine:

> Now they reign in heav'nly glory,
> Now they walk in golden light,
> Now they drink, as from a river,
> Holy bliss and infinite;
>
> Love and peace they taste for ever,
> And all truth and knowledge see
> In the beatific vision
> Of the blessèd Trinity.

Ellerton seems to have been instrumental in persuading his co-editors to restore this verse in the 1881 edition of *Church Hymns*. He wrote a lengthy note pointing out that this did not mean that he countenanced "the popular error that the Blessed are already in the full fruition of their future and everlasting glory". Rather, he argued, Wordsworth's verse "was to be regarded as the utterance in triumphant song of a vision of the final gathering of the Saints, not an exposition of their present condition in the intermediate state".[4]

In fact, Ellerton's other great funeral hymn, "Now the labourer's task is o'er", does contain a clear statement of the orthodox Christian doctrine of a long sleep after death preceding the general resurrection. It was written for *Church Hymns* in 1871, inspired by and loosely based on verses beginning "Brother, now thy toil is o'er", written by Gerard Moultrie, a prolific High Anglican hymnwriter, during his attendance at a Requiem Mass in Boulogne in 1863 and subsequently reworked as a hymn beginning "Now the labourer's toils are o'er". Ellerton considerably improved on the original while following its broad outline, although he took out Moultrie's lines about the reunion of friends in heaven:

> Friends and dear ones, gone before
> To the land of endless peace,
> Meet thee on that further shore
> Where all tears and sorrows cease.

Ellerton's "Now the labourer's task is o'er" was much more widely taken up than "God of the living", appearing in over 100 hymn books. Here is the text in full:

> Now the labourer's task is o'er;
> Now the battle day is past;
> Now upon the farther shore
> Lands the voyager at last.
>
> *Father, in Thy gracious keeping*
> *Leave we now Thy servant sleeping.*
>
> There the tears of earth are dried;
> There its hidden things are clear;
> There the work of life is tried
> By a juster Judge than here.
>
> There the Angels bear on high
> Many a strayed and wounded lamb,
> Peacefully at last to lie
> In the breast of Abraham.
>
> There the sinful souls, that turn
> To the cross their dying eyes,
> All the love of Christ shall learn
> At His feet in Paradise.
>
> There no more the powers of hell
> Can prevail to mar their peace;
> Christ the Lord shall guard them well,
> He Who died for their release.
>
> 'Earth to earth, and dust to dust,'
> Calmly now the words we say;
> Left behind, we wait in trust
> For the resurrection day.

Alongside the repeated refrain which hands the dead over to God's gracious keeping, there is much rich imagery in the above verses which echoes prominent themes found in other Victorian hymns and poems. The first verse employs the image of the voyager landing "upon the farther shore", expressing the idea of death as a casting-off into the sea on a journey to a distant shore, which is found in the poetry of Tennyson, Rossetti and many others.[5] The suggestion in the second verse that in heaven the tears of earth are dried and our lives judged by "a juster judge than here" echoes the sentiments expressed by Frederick William Faber in his hymn "Come to Jesus" published in 1854:

> There's a wideness in God's mercy,
> Like the wideness of the sea;
> There's a kindness in his justice
> Which is more than liberty.
>
> There is no place where earth's sorrows
> Are more felt than up in heaven:
> There is no place where earth's failings
> Have such kindly judgement given.

This comforting message is confirmed by the reference in the third verse of Ellerton's hymn to angels bringing "many a strayed and wounded lamb" to lie peacefully in the breast of Abraham. Ellerton later changed this verse to:

> There the Shepherd, bringing home
> Many a lamb forlorn and strayed,
> Shelters each, no more to roam,
> Where the wolf can ne'er invade.

In this revised version, there is a very explicit allusion to the idea of Christ as the Good Shepherd and the parable of the lost sheep. This was a common trope in Victorian hymnody, perhaps most explicitly found in Elizabeth Clephane's 1868 gospel song, "There were ninety and nine that safely lay in the shelter of the fold".

The fourth verse of Ellerton's hymn, with its reference to sinful souls turning their dying eyes to the cross, is reminiscent of the line "Hold thou thy cross before my closing eyes" in Henry Francis Lyte's "Abide With Me". In the fifth verse, Ellerton returns to the theme that he introduced in "God of the living" when he wrote of Jesus filling a human grave and so banishing our fears that we might not attain eternal life. Here there is an even more explicit affirmation that Jesus died to release the sinful souls trapped in hell. Ellerton is surely alluding here to the notion of Jesus' descent into hell after his own death to release the souls trapped there which, although not explicitly stated in the Bible, is hinted at in verses in the first epistle of Peter and the letter to the Ephesians and expressed in the line in the Apostles' Creed, "He descended into Hell". The belief being expressed in this verse, as in Ellerton's earlier funeral hymn, is that Jesus himself went through the experience not just of dying but of being dead. His soul joined those already dead in order to bring them with him into eternal life.

In many respects "Now the labourer's task is o'er" is highly orthodox—it accepts the notion of judgment, albeit by a more just and merciful judge than here on earth, and in its final line clearly posits the doctrine of a final resurrection day for which all souls, living and dead, must wait. Yet at the same time it has more than a hint of universalism. I am tempted to include it, too, in the list of hymns for my own funeral, but as there are so many others that I would like to have, I had probably better ration myself, or rather those who are there to send me off, to just one per author.

What John Ellerton provides in his two funeral hymns, so beautifully crafted and so evidently the products of a lifetime in parish ministry, is the Victorian Broad Church view of heaven with its universalist tendency and its emphasis on God's all-encompassing love and mercy from which no souls are exempt. Here is the gentle, reassuring touch of the faithful pastor who has sat at the bedside of many a dying parishioner. It is perfectly expressed in the second verse of his hymn "O Strength and Stay, upholding all creation":

> Grant to life's day a calm unclouded ending,
> An eve untouched by shadows of decay,
> The brightness of a holy death-bed blending
> With dawning glories of the eternal day.

## Notes

[1] Bernard Braley, *Hymnwriters*, Vol. 1 (London: Stainer & Bell, 1987), pp. 157–8.
[2] John Polkinghorne, "Eschatological Credibility: Emergent and Teleological Processes", in Robert Russell, Ted Peters and Michael Welker (eds), *Resurrection: Theological and Scientific Assessments* (Grand Rapids, MI: Eerdmans, 2002), p. 52.
[3] Charles Hartshorne, "Time, Death and Eternal Life", *The Journal of Religion* 95:4 (2015), p. 101.
[4] Braley, *Hymnwriters*, Vol. 1, pp. 181–2.
[5] For other examples of the use of this imagery, see Ian Bradley, *The Quiet Haven: An Anthology of Readings on Death and Heaven* (London: Darton, Longman & Todd, 2021), especially pp. 80–1, 110–11.

# 6

# "Rest without ceasing to work"

## F. D. Maurice

Frederick Denison Maurice (1805–72) made two highly significant contributions to Victorian thinking about heaven. In his *Theological Essays* of 1853, he seriously challenged the doctrine of everlasting punishment, which he took to be commonly accepted throughout the Church and more widely in society. Later, in a series of sermons and books published in the 1860s, he reflected deeply on the subject of the afterlife, emphasizing its qualitative rather than quantitative temporal nature, and envisaging heaven as a place of activity and effort rather than of rest.

His writings proved highly influential. Maurice was credited by several of his contemporaries as being instrumental in weakening the hold of the idea of everlasting punishment and damnation in the latter part of the nineteenth century, especially within the Church of England. He has also been seen by historians as one of the chief architects of the Victorian view of heaven as essentially a continuation of life on earth, involving the reunion of family and friends and the pursuit of tasks and self-improvement.

For me, Maurice is the greatest ever British theologian. His intellectual brilliance and breadth, expressed in nearly 40 books ranging from biblical exegesis through Christology to eschatology, was combined with a deep pastoral concern and active commitment to social and political reform. A pioneer Christian Socialist, he once remarked that he learned more theology in the wards of Guy's Hospital, London, during his time as chaplain there than from all the books in his study at nearby King's College, where he was professor of theology.

Born in 1805 in Suffolk, where his father was a Unitarian minister, he became an Anglican and was ordained deacon in 1834 and priest a year later. Although he forsook the denomination in which he had been reared, he never lost some of the central tenets of Unitarianism, notably its conception of God as a loving father and its association with political radicalism. He was attracted by the broad inclusive nature of Anglicanism and by what he saw as the capacity of an established church to spiritualize national life. His first major work, *The Kingdom of Christ*, first published in 1838, asserted the headship of Christ over all humanity, whereby everyone is incorporated into God's family and held in divine love. For Maurice, there is nothing and no one that Christ has not redeemed. This conviction underlay his approach to what happens after death and his attack on the Evangelical notion that humanity is divided into the saved and the irredeemably damned.

In 1853, he was dismissed from his chairs at King's College, where he was professor of English literature and history as well as of theology, for his apparent denial of the doctrine of eternal punishment in his *Theological Essays*. Challenging the prevailing Evangelical belief in an everlasting hell, he argued that God created human beings not to reward or punish them but to give them eternal life. Although he himself vehemently denied that he was a universalist, and conceded that some by their own choice consciously reject fellowship with God in Christ and through this deliberate alienation from God create their own hell and state of eternal loss, his teaching about the depth and breadth of God's love brought him very close to espousing a belief in universal salvation. He accepted that ultimately what happens after death is a mystery which we can never penetrate, but as he wrote in the concluding essay of his *Theological Essays*, entitled "Eternal Life and Eternal Death",

> I am obliged to believe in an abyss of love which is deeper than the abyss of death; I dare not lose faith in that love. I sink into death, internal death, if I do so. I must feel that this love is compassing the universe. More about it I cannot know. But God knows. I leave myself and all to Him.[1]

Maurice grounded his argument on two New Testament texts, St Paul's assertion in 1 Timothy 2:4 that "it is the will of God that all men should be saved" and St John's words in 1 John 4:16 that "God is love". He also drew on the writings of the early fathers, especially Origen, whose influence is clear in his prayer that finally "Christ would claim the last of his race" and that there would be no one left outside the scope of God's love and Christ's redemption. He refused to accept that those who die impenitent are lost forever and challenged the widespread view that those who do not accept God's salvation during this life are irretrievably lost. He also attacked what he called "the common view" that the vast majority of humankind are destined for eternal punishment and that only a small elect will enjoy the eternal joys of heaven.

The *Theological Essays* were dedicated to Tennyson and the preface ended by quoting from "In Memoriam" and expressing the hope that

> the bells of our church might indeed
> Ring out the darkness of the land,
> Ring in the Christ that is to be.

In the preface to the second edition, Maurice noted that he had written the essays to prevent "the doctrine, that an immense majority of our fellow-beings are in an utterly hopeless condition, from being regarded as *the characteristic* doctrine of Christian Divinity". "Multitudes of our Christian brethren", he suggested, "understand us to say that God has sent His Son into the world, not to save it, but to condemn it." He was particularly keen to reassure Unitarians, in whose liberal and universalist theology he had been reared, that "the Church of England gives not the faintest encouragement to so horrible a contradiction of God's word".[2]

The doctrines which Maurice attacked were widely held and preached by Evangelicals in both the Church of England and Nonconformist denominations in the early years of Victoria's reign. An article in the Unitarian *Christian Reformer* pointed out in 1840 that, according to one group of Calvinistically inclined Congregationalist theologians, the ratio of those who would be saved to those who would be damned eternally was in the order of 1:90. Hellfire preaching was also common among Anglo-Catholic and Roman Catholic clergy, with the infamous

Redemptorist priest, Father Joseph Furniss, terrorizing children through tracts described by one of their readers as "penny-dreadful word paintings of phosphorescent charnel-house horrors". The widespread dissemination of such ideas from pulpits and in popular tracts led to a pervasive fear among many churchgoers and beyond that most people would be damned and end up in the fiery, sulphurous streams of hell which resounded, in Furniss' words, "with the shrieks of millions and millions of tormented souls, roaring like lions, hissing like serpents, howling like dogs, and wailing like dragons".[3]

Maurice did not expect quick success in his efforts to turn the tide of public opinion on this subject. He observed in the preface to *Theological Essays* that "the hopes expressed in this volume are more likely to be fulfilled to our children than to ourselves".[4] In fact, his attack on the pervasive doctrine of everlasting punishment did have a considerable impact in his own lifetime, thanks partly to the fact that his dismissal from his chair at King's was widely publicized and, in Geoffrey Rowell's words, became "one of the theological *causes célèbres* of the nineteenth century".[5] Among the many people whose views were directly changed by his arguments was a prominent society lady, Charlotte Williams Wynn, who was in the throes of a nervous breakdown in 1858 because of her fear, stoked by evangelical teaching in her youth, that despite leading a blameless and charitable life devoted to the poor she would be damned, making her "thoroughly unhappy from the constant fear of the wrath of this inexorable Judge". She was cured by being given a volume of Maurice's sermons to read and being reassured by them "that God is a God of love, and that He does not punish in anger".[6]

Maurice's crusade to turn the Church of England in particular from promulgating the doctrine of everlasting punishment was greatly assisted by a number of Anglican disciples whom he recruited to the cause. They included John Colenso (see p. 10) and Henry Wilson, who was suspended from his living in Cambridgeshire for a year for denying the doctrine of eternal punishment in the celebrated collection of essays by Broad Church Anglicans published in 1860 under the title *Essays and Reviews*. The most devoted, and the most influential, of these disciples was Frederic William Farrar, who had been Maurice's student at King's College and went on to become an archdeacon, a canon of Westminster

Abbey and Dean of Canterbury Cathedral. In five sermons on "Eternal Hope" preached in Westminster Abbey in 1877, which subsequently became a bestselling book, he analysed what he regarded as the four prevalent views about what happened after death, beginning with

> The *Common* view, which, to the utter detriment of all noble thoughts of God, and to all joy and peace in believing, declares (i) that at death there is passed upon every impenitent sinner an irreversible doom to endless tortures, either material or mental, of the most awful and unspeakable intensity; and (ii) that this doom awaits the vast majority of mankind.

An alternative to this view was annihilationism or "conditional immortality" whereby the wicked would simply be destroyed. The third prevalent view Farrar explored was the idea of Purgatory, an intermediate state which allowed souls to be purified between death and judgment. The fourth position he described as "*Universalism*, or, as it is now sometimes termed, Restorationism: the opinion that all men will be ultimately saved".[7]

Although Farrar, like Maurice, strenuously denied that he was a universalist and maintained that some would not be saved, there was no doubt that he leaned strongly in this direction. As with Tennyson, his emphasis was on hope and like Maurice he felt that churches, and especially Protestant churches, had got the balance wrong in suggesting that heaven was the destination only for a minority of those who died and that the majority would go to hell. In seeking to right this imbalance, he was a pivotal figure in shifting mainstream opinion in the Church of England and beyond it in the nation in favour of a much greater focus on heaven than on hell and a much more hope-filled theology about the number of those who would end up there. This did not involve losing the sense of God as a judge or the notion of judgment after death, but it did mean much more emphasis on divine mercy than on divine wrath.

The fact that Farrar felt the need to preach and write on *Eternal Hope* nearly 25 years after the publication of Maurice's *Theological Essays* underlines that the weaning of Church of England clergy away from notions of eternal punishment was a slow and gradual process.

The growing assaults on the doctrine from Maurice's Broad Church disciples met with strong opposition from Evangelical and Tractarian clergy, 11,000 of whom (nearly half of the 24,000 clergy in the Church of England) signed a Litany in 1864 affirming that the Church of England believed and taught that "punishment of the cursed" was everlasting. However, as the century wore on, the grip of the doctrine of eternal punishment on both the Church of England and other denominations substantially weakened. By 1879, the essayist George Somers Bellamy could write, "Thank God, very few of us remain today who believe in 'endless punishment," and 20 years later W. E. Gladstone commented that the doctrine of hell had been "relegated . . . to the far-off corners of the Christian mind . . . there to sleep in deep shadow as a thing needless in our enlightened and progressive age".[8] Around the same time Stewart Headlam, an Anglican priest and prominent Christian Socialist who studied under Maurice at Cambridge and described him as the primary influence in his life, told a meeting of members of the Fabian Society that "they probably did not know what it was to have been delivered in the world of thought, emotion, imagination from the belief that a large proportion of the human race are doomed to eternal misery". He attributed this change of outlook primarily to Maurice's influence.[9]

Maurice did not just change his contemporaries' view as to how many of them would get to heaven. He also profoundly influenced their understanding of what it would be like when they got there. Arguing that heaven is a state of being and of relationship with God rather than a place, he felt that the concept of eternal life could only be understood by detaching it from any notion of temporality. Eternal life has nothing to do with time or duration. It consists of the knowledge of God. Our lives are the image of God's life and as such they are eternal—they did not begin at a certain time and they will not end at a certain time. Eternity is better expressed by a circle than by a line, being a quality of experience rather than a matter of temporal duration. To know God and to dwell in Christ is to experience eternal life and to live in heaven now, just as self-imposed separation from God is eternal death. Those who are bound for heaven are already in heaven because they love God. Eternal life is a future life begun in the present life and consisting of the knowledge of God.

These sentiments were strongly echoed by Maurice's devoted disciple, Frederic Farrar, who wrote about heaven in *Eternal Hope*: "Is it not a state rather than a place? Is it not *to be something* rather than *to go somewhere*? Yes, this, this is Heaven." He went on to state his strong conviction that heaven should not be thought of as "some meadow of asphodel beside the crystal waters, or golden city in the far-off blue".[10]

In many ways, Maurice and his followers anticipated the realized eschatology of many twentieth-century theologians with their emphasis on life here and now in this world rather than fruitless pie-in-the-sky speculation about life in the next one. Similar sentiments underlay his strenuous Christian Socialist call to bring about the kingdom of God and Christ by righting inequality and injustice, ending capitalism and competition and inaugurating a new reign of human co-operation.

While seeing heaven more as a state of being than a place, Maurice did at the same time conceive of it in quite concrete terms and wrote a good deal about what it might be like. His view of heaven, as worked out in a series of sermons and lectures in the 1850s and early 1860s, stands in marked contrast to the sentimental and static picture of angelic choruses endlessly strumming harps and singing hymns of praise presented in popular hymns, poems and sermons. He was uneasy about depicting it primarily as a state of passive rest. In a sermon on *Death and Life* (1855), he wrote about Paul's statement in 1 Thessalonians 4:14 that those "which sleep in Jesus will God bring with him":

> That is the rest which you were longing to claim for him, the termination of uneasy struggles, of doubts, of sufferings. But it is rest in Him from whom all his energies and activities were derived, in Him who was the secret spring of his soul's life and his body's life.[11]

In other words, the sleep that we are promised in Jesus is of a very active kind and as much like life as it is like death.

His most sustained meditation on the nature of heaven is contained in his 1861 *Lectures on the Apocalypse,* in which he exegeted the last book of the Bible, the Revelation to John, traditionally thought to have been written by a Christian from Ephesus known as John the Divine, possibly exiled on the island of Patmos at the end of the first century. Maurice takes John's Revelation to show that what happens in heaven is closely connected with what happens on earth—indeed in many ways life there is a continuation of life here. In his words, the kingdom of heaven "is indeed a real kingdom, not far off in some distant star" but "connected by common pursuits and interests with all that was passing here".[12] Like many of his contemporaries, he makes much of the worship that will take place in heaven, but for him this worship is intertwined with work, activity and growth in knowledge. As he describes it, heaven is a kind of Christian Socialist paradise in which "all are pursuing the highest good in contemplation and action" and working ceaselessly together in a spirit of co-operation:

> Oftentimes it has been said in Christian pulpits, that heaven is but the continuance of the worship upon earth. Those who have found that worship on earth very dreary and unsatisfactory have said that they would prefer any Greek Elysium or Gothic Valhalla to such a heaven. I think if we take St John as our guide—if we accept his revelation as the true revelation—we may see a meaning in the assertion of the divine, and a meaning in the protest of the layman. All is worship there, because all are pursuing the highest good in contemplation and action; because all are referring their thoughts and acts to one centre, instead of scattering and dispersing them by turning to a thousand different centres; because each thinker and each doer is forgetting himself in the object which he has before him, in the work which is committed to him...
> 
> The heavenly worship is continuous only because growth in knowledge is continuous, and because all free action is continuous. In the many mansions there is room for every form of life, only the shapes of death can be excluded...
> 
> I say, then, we have here the Christian Elysium, or Valhalla, or Paradise, that which you are all looking for when your thoughts are calmest and truest; when you are most tormented by the discords of the world around you, and of your own hearts; when you are most sure there must be a harmony without discords;

> when you long for scope to complete tasks which death will leave unfinished; when you wish to recover affections which have been broken; to know what you have been unable to know; to work bravely; to rest without ceasing to work.[13]

Alongside the insistence on the diversity of heaven, with its "room for every form of life" in its many mansions, what is particularly striking in the extract above is the emphasis at the end on heaven as a place of strenuous activity in which one can "complete tasks which death will leave unfinished ... work bravely and rest without ceasing to work". It is no coincidence that Maurice is depicted prominently in Ford Madox Brown's famous painting *Work*. He stands alongside Thomas Carlyle, another leading proponent of the Victorian Gospel of Work, as one of the two "brain workers" watching navvies and costermongers at their more physical labours. He was far from being the only nineteenth-century Protestant minister and theologian to depict heaven primarily in terms of the opportunities it offered for strenuous activity, development and of society and self. It was a favourite theme of those who, like him, came from the Unitarian fold. The American Unitarian minister William Channing preached in an Easter Sunday sermon in 1834:

> We must not think of Heaven as a stationary community. I think of it as a world of stupendous plans and efforts for its own improvement. I think of it as a society passing through successive stages of development, virtue, knowledge, power, by the energy of its own members. There the work of education, which began here, goes on without end; and a diviner philosophy than is taught on earth, reveals the spirit to itself, and awakens it to earnest, joyful effort for its own perfection.[14]

Several English Nonconformist divines shared this view of heaven. James Baldwin Brown, a liberal Congregationalist minister, intensely disliked the "restful and self-centred view of immortality" expressed in popular evangelical hymns, like this one that he singled out for particular opprobrium:

> There on a green and flowery mount
> Our weary souls shall sit,
> And with transporting joys recount
> The labours of our feet.

Baldwin Brown deplored this picture of selfish souls "mooning on the mount" and suggested that they should instead be set to "some good work for God and their world". Heaven, he believed, would promise "fruitful sunlit activity" based on truth, righteousness and love.[15]

Several eminent lay Christians took a similar view. Maurice's fellow Christian Socialist, Thomas Hughes, expressed it in his novel *Tom Brown's School Days,* in which the pious and sickly Arthur has a vision of the next world when he thinks that he is dying. He looks across the river of death and on the far bank "were a multitude which no man could number, and they worked at some great work; and they who rose from the river went on and joined in the work. They all worked, and each worked in a different way, but all at the same work."[16] Florence Nightingale had a similarly strenuous view of heaven. When Lady Stephen expressed her opinion that a mutual friend who had died "after a busy life" was now in a state of rest, "Miss Nightingale at once sat bolt upright. 'Oh, no' she said with conviction, 'I am sure it is an immense activity'".[17] William Ewart Gladstone believed in what he called "the progressive state of the Christian dead", while his clerical son-in-law, Harry Drew, Rector of Hawarden, looked forward to an afterlife of "endless bliss and infinite possibilities and capacities where every power shall have free and unimpeded development".[18]

In their book *Heaven: A History*, Bernhard Lang and Colleen McDannell note that around the middle of the nineteenth century the traditional, static, theocentric picture of heaven as a restful place filled by psalm-singing saints began to give way to a more dynamic view of a place of growth and activity. Increasingly, in the latter half of the century, "service and education replaced worship as the primary activity of the Protestant heaven".[19] While they credit the Victorian work ethic and idea of progress for this change, there is no doubt that the writings of Maurice and those influenced by him also played a part. By the end of the century, Anglican as well as Nonconformist clergy were taking up his idea of heaven as a state or place of strenuous activity and progressive development.

There was a deeper theological and philosophical aspect to this changing view of heaven. It was bound up with the increasing emphasis on the immortality of the soul rather than the resurrection of the body and with the widespread notion that the destiny of humanity was one of unending progress rather than arrival at a static state of perfection. Geoffrey Rowell has commented more generally about much nineteenth-century Christian eschatology:

> It was an immortality of self-realization, rather than an immortality of salvation, to which man looked forward, so we find that in many nineteenth-century works on eschatology the future life is envisaged as a time of ever-increasing powers of mind and knowledge of the universe, attendance at some celestial university.[20]

This idea of heaven as a progressive rather than a static state, characterized by strenuous activity, continuing human development and the gradual attainment of perfection was not new. It can be traced back to Origen, who envisaged souls ascending through various levels of celestial spheres, taught by "angelic instructors, who will teach them the answers to all the questions that puzzled them on earth". Most other medieval theologians, however, preferred to posit a static hereafter and their view was not really challenged until the eighteenth century when, among others, Jonathan Edwards, Joseph Addison and Isaac Watts argued that there must be movement and progress in heaven.

The notion of heaven as a kind of "celestial university" where souls would develop and become ever more enlightened became much more widespread in the nineteenth century. As one might expect, it was found particularly among Broad Church Anglicans and liberal Nonconformists. In *In Memoriam* Tennyson wrote of "the full-grown energies of heaven" and speculated that Arthur Hallam would change and progress there, leaving those mourning him on earth "evermore a life behind". Henry Wilson, who moved in 1850 from being Professor of Anglo-Saxon at Oxford to vicar of Great Staughton in Oxfordshire, and whose contribution to *Essays and Reviews* led to him being tried for heresy in the Court of Arches, saw heaven not so much as a university as a nursery where those who were infants "not as to years of terrestrial life, but as to spiritual development" would grow and "be quickened into higher life".[21] Samuel Cox, a Baptist minister who espoused universalist views, argued in a series of lectures published in book form as *Salvator Mundi* in 1877 that death did not mark a sudden and sharp break in human development, but was rather part of a gradual evolutionary progress that continued in the afterlife. Although Evangelicals and Tractarians tended to condemn such ideas, by the end of the century even some of them were coming round to espouse them. In a book entitled *After Death*, published in 1880, Herbert Luckock, a Tractarian canon at Ely Cathedral and principal of Ely Theological College, wrote:

> If it be admitted that the soul exists after death, and is conscious, it seems impossible to believe that it remains altogether unchanged... Conscious life by all analogy involves progress or retrogression... and is not progress, steadily advancing progress, a very law of God's kingdom?[22]

If F. D. Maurice undoubtedly played a part in influencing this change of view from a static to a progressive heaven, he also helped to encourage what became the widespread Victorian belief in the restoration of family ties and earthly friendships after death. For him, heaven was very clearly somewhere, as he put it in the extract quoted above, "to recover affections which have been broken". In a book he wrote in 1857 on the Gospel of John, which developed his conception of the kingdom of God as a family, he wrote of the raising of Lazarus, "I cannot read this story without feeling that, among those things in heaven and earth that are so to be restored, the sympathies and affections of the family are some of the chief."[23]

Once again, he was by no means alone in promoting this aspect of heaven. We have already noticed how strongly it was affirmed by Queen Victoria and her chaplains (pp. 13–15). It became increasingly commonly discussed as the century went on with Unitarians again being to the fore, like the nineteen-year-old Emma Lee, who wrote to console a friend on her father's death in 1870: "It takes away all the mystery and horror of the grave, to think that when we die we shall only pass from the loving hearts and arms here, to the arms of those who have gone before us."[24] The reunion of friends and family after death was widely looked forward to by lay Anglicans. It is the feature of heaven most often commented upon in the writings of the 55 predominantly upper- and upper middle-class Victorian families that form the source material for Pat Jalland's book *Death in the Victorian Family*. Some Anglican clergy were initially more hesitant about making much of it, although others had no such qualms and Charles Kingsley even suggested that sexual relations continued or resumed in heaven. When Archibald Tait, by now Archbishop of Canterbury, lost both his wife Catharine and his son Crauford in 1879, Charles Ellicott, Bishop of Gloucester, wrote expressing his deep trust "in the abiding nature of the blessed family bond" which he felt was not emphasized enough in the Church's teaching.[25]

F. D. Maurice's view of heaven as essentially an extension of life on earth was hugely influential in helping to create the widespread Victorian belief that death would be like a homecoming with friends and family reunited and familiar tasks awaiting. In a lecture in 2009 on his legacy, delivered in the chapel of Trinity College, Cambridge, where Maurice had been an undergraduate, Boyd Hilton, the distinguished historian of Victorian Britain, summed up his influence thus:

> I'm going to caricature now: what follows isn't remotely in Maurice but it is what Maurice led people to think—Heaven was reconceptualized as a cosy domestic Dickensian fireside where the dead are reunited with all their old chums. Even the favourite old sock that they'd eventually had to throw away would be there awaiting them in its pre-darned state.[26]

This is a caricature, of course. Maurice's heaven was about much more than being reunited with favourite old socks. It was about continuing in the relationship with God that exists in this life. Heaven is the acknowledgement of and continued growing into that relationship, just as hell is the conscious rejection of it. Maurice was not without his doubts about what followed death and he hugely sympathized with the tentative and faint trust in the larger hope expressed in Tennyson's *In Memoriam* But he never lost faith in that "abyss of love which is deeper than the abyss of death" which he wrote about in his *Theological Essays* that caused so much controversy. He suffered doubts and fears on his own death bed before finally affirming, "I am not going to *Death* . . . I am going into *Life!*"[27]

## Notes

[1] Frederick Denison Maurice, *Theological Essays*, 2nd edn (London: Macmillan, 1853), p. 476.
[2] Maurice, *Theological Essays*, pp. xx–xxi.
[3] Geoffrey Rowell, *Hell and the Victorians: A Study of the Nineteenth-century Theological Controversies concerning Eternal Punishment and the Future Life* (Oxford: Clarendon Press, 1974), p. 172.
[4] Maurice, *Theological Essays*, p. v.
[5] Rowell, *Hell and the Victorians*, p. 62.
[6] "Frederick Denison Maurice, An address by Boyd Hilton", Trinity College Chapel, 1 November 2009, p. 7 at <http://trinitycollegechapel.com/media/filestore/sermons/HiltonMaurice011109.pdf>, accessed 10 March 2023.
[7] Frederic W. Farrar, *Eternal Hope* (London: Macmillan, 1878), p. xviii.
[8] George Somers Bellamy, *Essays from Shakespeare* (Edinburgh: Edinburgh Publishing Company, 1879), pp. 15–16; W. E. Gladstone, *Studies Subsidiary to the Works of Bishop Butler* (Oxford: Clarendon Press, 1898), p. 206.
[9] Frederick George Bettany, *Stewart Headlam: A Biography* (London: John Murray, 1925), p. 20.
[10] Farrar, *Eternal Hope*, pp. 19, 25.
[11] Frederick Denison Maurice, *Death and Life* (London: Macmillan, 1855), p. 11.
[12] Frederick Denison Maurice, *Lectures on the Apocalypse*, 3rd edn (London: Macmillan, 1893), p. 65.
[13] Maurice, *Lectures on the Apocalypse*, pp. 63–5.
[14] *The Works of William E. Channing*, Vol. IV (Boston: American Unitarian Association, 1903), p. 234.

15  J. Baldwin Brown, "The Soul and Future Life", *Nineteenth Century* 2 (October 1877), pp. 511–17.
16  Thomas Hughes, *Tom Brown's School Days* (London: Macmillan, 1869), p. 318.
17  Cecil Woodham-Smith, *Florence Nightingale, 1820–1910* (London: Constable, 1950), pp. 590–1.
18  Quoted in Pat Jalland, *Death in the Victorian Family* (Oxford: Oxford University Press, 1996), p. 269.
19  Colleen McDannell and Bernhard Lang, *Heaven: A History* (New Haven: Yale University Press, 2001), p. 287.
20  Rowell, *Hell and the Victorians*, p. 15.
21  Rowell, *Hell and the Victorians*, pp. 116–17.
22  Herbert Mortimer Luckock, *After death: An examination of the testimony of primitive times respecting the state of the faithful dead, and their relationship to the living* (London: Rivingtons, 1880), p. 36.
23  Frederick Denison Maurice, *The Gospel of John* (Cambridge: Macmillan, 1857), p. 318.
24  Jalland, *Death in the Victorian Family*, p. 275.
25  Jalland, *Death in the Victorian Family*, p. 275.
26  "F. D. Maurice: Address by Boyd Hilton", p. 8.
27  Frederick Maurice (ed.), *The Life of Frederick Denison Maurice*, Vol. II, 2nd edn (London: Macmillan, 1884), p. 641.

# 7

# "I give Thee back the life I owe, that in Thine ocean's depths its flow may richer, fuller be"

## George Matheson

George Matheson (1842–1906), the blind Church of Scotland minister now best known for "O love that will not let me go", the favourite hymn of both Margaret Thatcher and Arthur Scargill, thought and wrote much about death and immortality and what life in heaven might be like. Perhaps his most striking image, found in the opening verse of that hymn, is of the ocean depths of God's love in which the departed soul may find not just rest but also a richer and fuller life. It is an image that resonates with much Victorian imagining about what follows death and also with the way in which the afterlife has been conceived by both Christian and non-Christian mystics over the centuries. Douglas Davies singles it out in his book *The Theology of Death* as "a fine description of a believer who, amidst weariness, feels held by the divine love and whose sense of life is of a gift that now can be returned to the divine giver. The longing for depth, richness and fullness is seen to be part of the divine ocean". For Davies, it is of particular importance in respect of attitudes to death in showing that "when the longing for God is realized, in some measure, in this life, it becomes integrally related to a belief in an afterlife".[1]

Matheson did, indeed, believe that immortality was encountered in this life and was not something that only began with death. This led him to downplay the idea of resurrection perhaps more than any other Victorian Christian writer. In the words of Scott McKenna, his most recent biographer, "In a remarkable departure from orthodoxy, Matheson said that it is through union with God, oneness with the immortal spirit, that our immortality is secured: the concept of resurrection is meaningless."[2] Alongside his radical musings on the subject of immortality, Matheson also wrestled with the question of individual survival after death in several of his penetrating spiritual meditations, each triggered by a Bible verse, collected together in eight books which appeared between 1882 and his death in 1906 and became bestsellers.

Matheson's view of eternal life was part of a broad, liberal theological outlook, mystical in character and embracing a particular openness to other religions, developed in the aftermath of a severe crisis of faith which he suffered shortly after going to his first parish, Innellan on the Clyde coast, following his ordination in 1868. In his own words, "I found myself an absolute atheist. I believe nothing, neither God nor immortality."[3] He tendered his resignation to his fellow ministers in the local presbytery, but they wisely refused to accept it, telling him that he was a young man and would change his views. In fact, he came out of his period of spiritual darkness through reading the work of Hegel and Schleiermacher, espousing the philosophy of German idealism and embracing the findings of German biblical critics and theologians. From them he gained a strong sense of the comprehensiveness of Christianity and its underlying unity, purpose and order in terms of the working out of a *geist* or spirit. Its essential and defining character was to be found not in its creeds or dogma, still less in the authority of the Church and its rituals, but rather in the spiritual principle of eternal consciousness which manifested itself especially in self-sacrifice. The overriding *zeitgeist* running through the whole of creation and the whole of history was the spirit of sacrifice, embodied in the figure of Jesus Christ, the lamb slain from the foundation of the world. Much of Matheson's subsequent writing explored the theme of sacrifice, including the closing verse of his best-known hymn:

> O Cross that liftest up my head,
> I dare not ask to fly from thee.
> I lay in dust, life's glory dead,
> and from the ground there blossoms red,
> life that shall endless be.

Explaining the meaning of the last two lines, he wrote, "I took red as the symbol of that sacrificial life which blooms by shedding itself."[4]

Matheson became a nationally renowned preacher and devotional author despite being completely blind from the age of 18. His blindness profoundly affected his spirituality and mysticism—he wrote much about finding God in the shadows and in the darkness—and it also led him to develop and enhance his memory and his other senses, especially his hearing. A local doctor's recollections of an evening spent with him in the manse at Innellan illustrate just how much he used his hearing to stimulate his imagination and anticipation of heaven. A strong breeze was blowing over the Clyde, throwing up white horses that broke on the shore with a muffled roar, and a steamer was sounding its horn as it passed down the water. Standing by the window, the blind minister commented to his companion: "That weird music comes up here from the ocean like the far-off music of another world, a Symphony of great nature with the occasional syren note... Heaven sometimes begins here, and immortality."[5]

Matheson was not the only Scottish Presbyterian minister to feel that heaven began on the shores of the west coast. Standing one summer's day at Crinan harbour looking out from the great flats of the Mòine Mhór "steeped in the shimmering light of the west" to the islands in the Sound of Jura and beyond to the western ocean, Thomas Ratcliffe Barnett, a Free Church minister and inveterate pilgrim through Argyll, reflected:

> You may think you have come to a cul-de-sac of the world. But, before long, you will be quite sure that where the world ends heaven only begins... When the sun goes down in all its glory, the outgait to the west from Loch Crinan is like the forecourt of heaven.[6]

For Matheson, as indeed for Barnett, this was not just poetic fancy and imagining. He really did believe that heaven and immortality begin here in this life and not after death. It is the spirit of God within us that assures us of our immortality, which is something we gain in life rather than at death. In his *Natural Elements of Revealed Theology*, he emphasized what he took to be a major difference between Christianity and the doctrines of both Platonism and eastern religions. In the latter, dissolution of the body leads to the liberation of the soul "and the hour of death is the harbinger of the spiritual life". By contrast,

> Christian immortality is not a life which death brings to the soul, it is a life which belongs to the soul and which, therefore, death is unable to destroy. The continuity of life in this system is never for a moment broken. Death introduces no pause in the march of human existence; it is simply jostled out of the way in its attempt to oppose its march. The immortality exists within the soul as its birthright, not merely outside the soul as its destiny.[7]

Immortality for Matheson is not something that awaits us "in some far off and unknown future". Rather, humans are assured of immortality through union with the eternal through Christ. It is this belief that makes him somewhat dismissive of the Christian notion of resurrection, as is clear from the way that he treats the Gospel story of the raising of Lazarus in his *Studies in the Portrait of Christ*. For most commentators, Jesus' actions are interpreted as a miracle, raising a dead man to life, and as a kind of prequel to his own resurrection. Matheson takes a rather different view, giving Jesus these words to say to Martha:

> You call death the suspension of life. No, it is the transition of life. I am come to tell you, to show you, that the soul need not wait for the last day—that it can rise from the very bed of death, from the very couch of physical decay, from the very first touch of the hand of corruption. I am come to replace your thought of resurrection by my thought of immortality.[8]

This radical statement in which Jesus clearly identifies himself with the idea of immortality rather than that of resurrection is reinforced when Matheson goes on to say:

> Jesus was not immortal because He rose; He rose because He was immortal. The secret of His immortality was in Himself, not in His resurrection. He loosed the pains of death because He was

Himself stronger than death. That strength is our hope of glory. Easter is merely a manifestation of that strength—an effect of it, a result of it. Christ is, in the deepest sense, the cause of His own rising; in Christ, and not in His rising, lies our vision of immortality.⁹

In this understanding, Jesus' resurrection, and indeed the whole concept of resurrection, certainly as traditionally understood in Christianity, becomes somewhat superfluous. Indeed, Matheson goes so far as to say that "if a new and earlier Bible were found which closed its record at the cross of Calvary, I should still feel that in this portrait of the Son of Man I had the highest possible incidence of the existence of a soul invulnerable to death."¹⁰

In many ways, these are revolutionary sentiments which seem greatly to downplay the significance of the empty tomb, the post-resurrection appearances of Jesus and other features of the Gospel stories which have been the central grounds for Christian belief in life beyond death. Matheson rather wants to ground it in our relationship with God. He goes right back to the creation and the breathing of life into all creatures by God. It is by that breath that we are victors over death. In a prayer from a meditation on "The Ground for Immortality", he asks God:

> Teach me that the state after death exists already before death, that I need not taste of death until I have seen the Kingdom of God. Teach me that my immortality is not to come, that it is here, that it is now. Teach me that the life eternal is not merely the life *beyond* the grave, but the life on this side of the grave. Reveal to me that I am now in eternity, that I am breathing the very air of those that have passed the gates ... Let me feel that I am already immortal; that death could no more destroy *my* life than it could destroy Thine, because mine is Thine.¹¹

As well as greatly downplaying the idea of resurrection, Matheson also seems to cast grave doubt on the notion of the soul sleeping until a day of judgment. In a meditation on death, he writes: "The spirit cannot die, whether in or out of the body. Do not believe in the sleep of the soul;

the soul never sleeps. Even in the watches of the night it is the body and not the soul that slumbers. The sleep of death is like the sleep of life; it belongs to the weary frame, not to the living spirit."[12] He emphasizes this point by turning the tables on Tennyson and replacing the poet laureate's well-known line in his poem "The Brook" that "men may come and men may go, but I go on forever" with his own preferred version, "Brooks may come and brooks may go, but the soul goes on for ever."

It is in the context of these beliefs that we should approach the opening verse of Matheson's ever-popular hymn:

> O Love that wilt not let me go,
> I rest my weary soul in thee;
> I give thee back the life I owe,
> that in thine ocean depths its flow
> may richer, fuller be.

This envisaging of death as the return or surrender of the soul to the ocean depths of God's love is a familiar one in Victorian sacred literature. John Keble's hymn "Sun of My Soul, Thou Saviour Dear" ends with the lines "Till in the ocean of thy love, we lose ourselves in heaven above." John Trevor, a Unitarian minister who formed the Labour Church in 1891, wrote in his 1897 book *My Quest for God* of being "immersed in the infinite ocean of God". More broadly, the sea or ocean was widely used as a metaphor and image for death and what lies beyond, perhaps nowhere more poignantly and powerfully than in Charles Dickens' novel *Dombey and Son* (1848). The death of Fanny Dombey is described thus: "She drifted out upon the dark and unknown sea that rolls round all the world." The moving chapter describing young Paul Dombey's final illness and death is entitled "What the Waves are Saying" and describes the young boy's sensation of being carried down by a great rolling river into the sea. At the end, "the boat was out at sea, but gliding smoothly on". The chapter ends, "Thank God . . . for Immortality! And look upon us, angels of young children, when the swift river bears us to the ocean!"[13]

In an interesting article in the *Journal for Maritime Research*, Kirsty Read comments that "the sea itself played a more important role in Victorian cultures of death, dying and mourning than has hitherto been recognised".[14] She quotes an article published in the shipboard newspaper *The Pioneer*, produced during the voyage of the emigrant ship *Queen of the Thames* from Plymouth to Melbourne in 1864, which muses on the parallels between the ocean and heaven:

> 'The ocean has before now been likened to eternity with respect to its vastness' the writer remarked, but like heaven it was also a source of many treasures. Just as men dived for pearls in the sea, 'thus will it be in Heaven' when the 'Christian will be ever diving down into the depths of God's love, for fresh treasures.' 'Lastly', the article concluded, 'the ocean is like Heaven because of its purity.'[15]

Part of the reason why this oceanic metaphor for heaven became so popular in the nineteenth century was the increasing number of people who were buried at sea when they died. As Kirsty Read points out, "In an age of mass emigration, unprecedented numbers of people were on the move and, although maritime rates of mortality were in decline, deaths en route were still a common enough experience."[16] Burials at sea became a favourite subject for journalists, novelists, poets, painters, hymnwriters and moralists. In his poem "The Sailor's Grave", which was set to music by Arthur Sullivan and became a popular parlour ballad, Henry Lyte, the Anglican clergyman best known as the author of "Abide With Me" and "Praise My Soul, the King of Heaven", uses the imagery of the ocean as a perfect place for the long sleep of death (which, unlike Matheson, he believes to be the prelude to a general day of resurrection):

> Down, down, within the deep ...
> Sleep on, thou mighty dead!
> A glorious tomb they've found thee
> The broad blue sky above thee spread,
> The boundless waters round thee ...
> And when the last trump shall sound,
> And tombs are asunder riv'n,
> Like the morning sun from the wave thou'lt bound,
> To rise and shine in Heaven.[17]

It was not just in Britain that the connection between the sea and eternal life was made in the mid-nineteenth century. The French poet Charles Baudelaire (1821–67) mused: "Why is the spectacle of the sea so infinitely and eternally agreeable? Because the sea presents at once the idea of immensity and movement."[18] In "The Golden Legend" (1851), the medieval romance that was part of a trilogy entitled *Christus: A Mystery*, the American poet Henry Wadsworth Longfellow portrays Prince Henry of Hoheneck gazing out from the terrace of an inn on the coast at Genoa and experiencing a reverie not unlike Matheson's prompted by the sounds of the Clyde:

> It is the sea, it is the sea,
> In all its vague immensity,
> Fading and darkening in the distance!
> Silent, majestical, and slow,
> The white ships haunt it to and fro,
> With all their ghostly sails unfurled,
> As phantoms from another world
> Haunt the dim confines of existence!
> But ah! how few can comprehend
> Their signals, or to what good end
> From land to land they come and go!
> Upon a sea more vast and dark
> The spirits of the dead embark,
> All voyaging to unknown coasts.
> We wave our farewells from the shore,
> And they depart, and come no more,
> Or come as phantoms and as ghosts.[19]

The American poet Walt Whitman was especially fond of using the image of the sea in connection with death to describe God's all-encompassing eternal love. It is particularly vividly expressed in "On the Beach at Night Alone", a poem from the 1856 edition of his collection *Sea Drift* which was incorporated by Ralph Vaughan Williams into *A Sea Symphony*:

> On the beach at night alone,
> As the old mother sways her to and fro singing her husky song,
> As I watch the bright stars shining, I think a thought of the clef of the universes and of the future.
> A vast similitude interlocks all,
> All distances of place however wide,
> All distances of time,
> All souls, all living bodies though they be ever so different,
> All nations,
> All identities that have existed or may exist.
> All lives and deaths, all of the past, present, future,
> This vast similitude spans them, and always has spann'd,
> And shall forever span them and compactly hold and enclose them.[20]

This theme is echoed in a later poem in Whitman's *Passage to India* (1871):

> O soul thou pleasest me, I thee,
> Sailing these seas or on the hills, or waking in the night,
> Thoughts, silent thoughts, of Time and Space
>     and Death, like waters flowing,
> Bear me indeed as through the regions infinite,
> Whose air I breathe, whose ripples hear, lave me all over,
> Bathe me O God in thee, mounting to thee,
> I and my soul to range in range of thee.[21]

This poem ends with a call to the soul to venture into deeper and deeper waters, reassured by the understanding that they are "the seas of God":

> Sail forth—steer for the deep waters only,
> Reckless O soul, exploring, I with thee, and thou with me,
> For we are bound where mariner has not yet dared to go,
> And we will risk the ship, ourselves and all.
> O my brave soul!
>
> O farther farther sail!
> O daring joy, but safe! are they not all the seas of God?[22]

So Matheson was far from being alone among his contemporaries in imagining what happens after death as a journey of the soul into the ocean depths of God's love. This imagery is also found in the writings of both Christian and non-Christian mystics across the ages. The fourth-century ascetic Evagrius Ponticus uses the analogy of rivers flowing back to the sea to represent being "absorbed into God" and regaining lost union with the divine. The ninth-century Irish Neo-Platonist John Scotus Eriugena describes the divine nature in terms of "the sea of infinite goodness ready to give itself to those wishing to participate in it". The late-thirteenth-century German mystic Meister Eckhart envisages God as "a sea of infinite substance". In a similar vein, Rumi, the thirteenth-century Persian poet and Sufi mystic, calls on his readers to "give yourself up without regret and in exchange gain the ocean. In the arms of the sea you will be secure". Pointing out that "you are not a drop in the ocean. You are the entire ocean in a drop," he urges, "Plunge into the ocean of consciousness. Let the drop of water that is you become a hundred mighty seas." Bahá'u'lláh, the nineteenth-century founder of the Bahá'í faith, uses similar language, asking the "Lord of all names" to "lead me unto the ocean of Thy presence".[23]

There are echoes of Matheson's oceanic imagery in the prayers of the twentieth-century Scottish theologian John Baillie, as when he asks God "to drown my sin in the sea of your infinite love".[24] It is also perhaps worth remarking that many near-death experiences involve the sensation of either floating on or being absorbed into water. One such recorded in 2011 describes floating through the heavens, which become one with the sea:

> At first it was like looking at the sky, but as it became one with the sea, it was more like a translucent river of stars and colours, they would breeze and undulate. They seemed to be as one. They interacted like an ocean with the tide, with waves rising and falling lazily in space. I became aware of my place among them. I floated and relaxed.[25]

What makes Matheson's use of this common imagery to describe the post-mortem state particularly interesting is that he goes on to wrestle in his scriptural meditations with the vexed question as to whether souls are absorbed into the infinity of the ocean or retain their own individuality. His language in the opening verse of "O Love That Wilt Not Let Me Go" could be taken as suggesting the disappearance of the individual personality at death as it becomes merged with the infinite like a drop of water dissolving in the sea. He emphatically does not believe that this is what happens, however. In his 1884 meditation "On the Preservation of Personality in Heaven" on the biblical text "That God may be all in all" (1 Corinthians 15:28), he makes clear his belief that the human personality does not simply melt into the being of God as a cloud melts into the blaze of sunshine. Rather, it gains more brightness from being part of God's "sunshine's blaze":

> Am I, then, to be lost in God? Is my whole personal life to be absorbed and overshadowed in the life of the Infinite One? Am I to have no more separate being than one of those myriad drops which compose the vast ocean? If so, then my goal is death indeed. If my personality is to melt into the being of God as a cloud melts into the blaze of sunshine, then, surely, is God not my life but my annihilation. He can no longer say of me, 'Because I live, thou shalt live also.'
>
> Nay, but, my soul, thou hast misread the destiny of thy being. It is not merely written that God is to be all, but that He is to be all in all. His universal life is not to destroy the old varieties of being; it is to pulsate through these varieties. His music is to fill the world, but it is to sound through all the varied instruments of the world. His sunshine is to flood the universe, but it is to be mirrored in a thousand various forms.
>
> His love is to penetrate creation, but it is to be reflected in the infinite diversities of the hearts and souls of men.
>
> Thou speakest of losing thyself in the ocean of His love, but this is only poetically true.
>
> Love is an ocean where no man permanently loses himself; he regains himself in richer, nobler form. The only ocean in which a man loses himself is self-love; God's love gives him back his life that he may keep it unto life eternal.[26]

While Matheson is definite about the survival of the individual personality after death, he insists that this involves an abandonment of the ego with his reminder that "the only ocean in which a man loses himself is self-love". In taking this line, he is following Friedrich Schleiermacher, the founding father of nineteenth-century liberal theology, who defined the word devotion as "a losing of self in the infinite". It is loss of ego and of self-love which will indeed define the heavenly condition. In a meditation on the biblical text "Shall not the day of the Lord be darkness and not light?" (Amos 5:20), written shortly before his own death, Matheson suggests that there is no need to posit a separate heaven and hell. For the selfish, heaven will be a miserable place. "To a selfish man there would be no place in the universe so miserable as heaven. What makes heaven day to Jesus would make it night to Judas—the reign of love." His own fear is not that he will be excluded from heaven but rather that because of his own failings he may find it uncongenial:

> I fear to stand by the crystal river and have no eye for its clearness. I dread to walk in the green pastures and have no sense of their richness. I am afraid to be at the concert of multitudinous voices and have no ear for their sweetness. I tremble to be enrolled in the league of pity and have no heart for its kindness. Save me, O Father, from an uncongenial heaven![27]

But having made this important caveat about heaven being hell for the selfish and insensitive, Matheson goes on to suggest that it is a haven for free spirits and a place where we can exercise the full individuality which is denied to us on earth through the tyranny of uniformity and conformity. In his meditation on "Individual Immortality" based on the text "To every seed its own body" (1 Corinthians 15:38), he posits heaven as the home of the unconventional, the spontaneous and the free, distinguished by the difference rather than the sameness of its inhabitants:

> I heard an eminent theologian once say that, in his opinion, when we get to heaven we shall all think the same thing at the same time. This was his notion of reconciling the individual with

the universal. I should call it the killing of the individual by the universal. In such a state we might have communion with God, but we should never have communion with one another. What is it that makes the communion between any two souls? It is their mutual exchange of ideas. To think the same thing at the same time is not to exchange ideas.

Our separateness is not our sameness, but our communion. Communion demands difference—individuality. If you and I meet on the road some day and both exclaim in a breath, 'It is very fine weather', what have we given to each other? Nothing; we have simply expressed ourselves, uttered our united opinion. There is a great deal too much of this in the present world—union without communion. God says He will make it different yonder—a man will keep his own. Heaven will restore the individuality which earth has broken.

Lord, I have heard men say that death will rob me of my personal life. But Thou hast told me it is this world that robs me and that death will restore it. Here, I have not my own body; I have the body of the community; I am wound up to speak the same words that the world speaks. But yonder, I shall be an individual soul—unconventional, spontaneous, free.[28]

It is clear from the above that Matheson sees heaven as a place of intense sociability and, indeed, of vigorous debate and expression of personal views and opinions. In this, he echoed thoughts expressed three decades earlier by a fellow Church of Scotland minister, Norman Macleod, whom we have already come across preaching about heaven to Queen Victoria (see p. 14). Macleod was a major contributor to a book entitled *Recognition of Friends in Heaven* edited by Robert Bickersteth, Bishop of Ripon, and published in 1866. Beginning from the premise that "Man is a social being. We are made for brotherhood", Macleod goes on to argue that this sociability will continue in heaven and to invite his readers to "consider what ample resources heaven affords for the cultivation of the social affections among those of the highest intellect, and taste, and moral worth in God's universe". Like Matheson, he comes down firmly in terms of preservation of individual identity: "There is no reason whatever to doubt, that each person shall retain marked individual features of mind, and peculiarities of character, there as well as here. All the stars will shine in brilliancy, and sweep in orbits more or less wide around the great centre, but each star will differ from another star in glory." MacLeod concludes: "I cannot really understand how anyone should doubt . . . the recognition of our Christian friends in heaven. As well ask me to prove this, as to prove that I should recognize them if we met in a different part of the country next week, after having been separated from them only for a few days."[29]

If Matheson is very much with his fellow Victorians in emphasizing the reuniting of friends and family in heaven, he goes rather further than many of them in his envisioning of the liveliness and spiritedness of their interactions. There is also for him a theocentric dimension to this interaction. It is achieved through God. In a posthumously published meditation inspired by Psalm 139, verses 9 and 10 ("If I take the wings of the morning, and dwell in the uttermost parts of the sea; even there . . . Thy right hand shall hold me"), which picks up the image of the sea symbolizing death, he posits a brotherhood on earth and a brotherhood in heaven and argues that they are connected through God:

> The greatest comfort to all hours of separation is the idea of God. When you are to be divided from a friend by an earthly sea there can be no deeper solace than the thought that you and he are to be really within the hollow of a single hand—that, while unable to touch one another, you will be in the presence of one who is touching you both. And when there comes the separation of that widest sea—death, there is again no solace so deep as that. At such a time what do I want to know? Is it whether the streets of heaven are paved with gold, is it whether the songs of heaven are rich in music, is it whether the work of heaven is wrought by angels? It is none of these things. It is whether in this vast universe beyond the earth there is anything which can connect my life with the life of my departed brother. What a comfort to be told that, with all our seeming separation, we are still inmates of the same house—the House of God! That is just what the psalmist says. He says that absolute separation between two souls is an

impossibility—that the wings of the morning can never lift us outside the gates of God.[30]

So Matheson sees heaven as a place where individuality, however "unconventional, spontaneous and free", can flourish and at the same time where souls are brought together rather than separated. He expresses this latter aspect vividly in a meditation on the statement in Revelation 21:1 that in the new heaven and new earth there is no longer any sea. He takes this to be an allusion to the fact that in this life we are "a multitude of little islands divided by stormy waves" whereas in the life to come "the gulfs are all dried up" and human life becomes a connected continent.[31]

The image of the sea with its vastness and ocean depths features yet again in another wonderfully rich meditation which sums up George Matheson's view of heaven. Written in 1895 and entitled "On the Preparation of Humanity's Dwelling-Place", it is inspired by the familiar text of John 14:2: "In My Father's house are many mansions ... I go to prepare a place for you." He begins by picturing our individual lives moving in a vast sea and seeming to be mere specks amid the waves as we wonder what lies at the end of the universe. What is important is who rather than what awaits us after death, not gorgeous furniture but rather something more homely—"an old glance of the eye, an old ring of the voice, an old clasp of the hand". As in the meditation quote above, he has no interest in the golden streets, pearly gates and sapphire thrones promised in the Book of Revelation. Rather he wants "the sympathy of a brother's soul". In many ways, like Maurice and so many other Victorians, he is here envisaging heaven as an extension of life on earth, not least in its familiar and homely aspects. Above all he is comforted by the fact that Jesus has gone there before us to prepare the way. "I cannot get that place by going over the bridge; I can only get it by someone going over before me. What I want is a heart already there."

> Often have I been startled by the vastness of that sea in which my little life is moving; I seem but a speck amid myriad waves. I want to know what is at the end of the universe. Is there a human soul there? Is there anything that can respond to my spirit? Is there aught that can love when I love, weep when I weep, joy when I

joy? Is there a pulse of sympathy that can answer to the pulse of my heart? Is there a place prepared for me? I cannot get that place by going over the bridge; I can only get it by someone going over before me. What I want is a heart already there, a kindred soul to meet me, a human life to greet me. The 'going before' is itself the 'preparing'.

I want no gorgeous furniture in my room of the Father's house. I am afraid the furniture may be too gorgeous. I want something homely—like home. I seek an old glance of the eye, an old ring of the voice, an old clasp of the hand. I seek the ancient sympathy that has linked man to man, the earthly love that has knit heart to heart, the human trust that has bound life to life. I seek in eternity the image of time; that is the place I would have prepared for me.

Let not thy heart be troubled; in the vast spaces there is a home for thee. The Son of Man has gone before; there is a region prepared for humanity. There is a spot in this stupendous universe where human nature dwells. That spot is thy one comfort, thy one glory. No other glory would make up for it. There may be golden streets and pearly gates and sapphire thrones. There may be rivers clear as crystal, and trees rich in foliage, and flowers full of bloom. There may be suns that never set, and hands that never weary, and lives that never die. But about these many things thy heart is not troubled. One thing is needful, without which all were vain—the sympathy of a brother's soul.[32]

## Notes

[1] Douglas Davies, *The Theology of Death* (Edinburgh: T&T Clark, 2008), p. 98.
[2] Scott McKenna, *George Matheson and Mysticism: A Biographical Study* (Eugene, OR: Pickwick Publications, 2022), p. 16.
[3] Donald Macmillan, *The Life of George Matheson* (London: Hodder & Stoughton, 1901), p. 121.

4   Ian Bradley, *O Love that wilt not let me go* (London: Collins Fount, 1990), pp. 39–40.
5   Macmillan, *Life of Matheson*, pp. 284–5.
6   Thomas Ratcliffe Barnett, *The Land of Lorne* (Edinburgh: Chambers, 1933), p. 144.
7   George Matheson, *Natural Elements of Revealed Theology* (London: J. Nisbet, 1881), p. 174.
8   George Matheson, *Studies in the Portrait of Christ*, Vol. II (London: Hodder & Stoughton, 1901), p. 157.
9   Matheson, *Studies in the Portrait of Christ*, p. 334.
10  Matheson, *Studies in the Portrait of Christ*, p. 335.
11  George Matheson, *Moments on the Mount* (London: J. Nisbet, 1884), p. 48.
12  Matheson, *Moments on the Mount*, pp. 247–8.
13  Charles Dickens, *Dombey and Son* (London: J. M. Dent, 1907), p. 212.
14  Kirsty Read, "Ocean Funerals: The Sea and Victorian Cultures of Death", *Journal for Maritime Research* 23:1 (2011), p. 38.
15  Read, "Ocean Funerals", p. 46.
16  Read, "Ocean Funerals", p. 47.
17  H. F. Lyte and Arthur S. Sullivan, *The Sailor's Grave* (London: J. B. Cramer & Co., 1872).
18  Alev Lytle Croutier, *Taking the Waters: Spirit, Art, Sensuality* (New York: Abbeville Press, 1992), p. 50.
19  Henry Longfellow, *The Golden Legend* (Boston: Houghton, Mifflin & Co., 1887), p. 161.
20  Walt Whitman, *Leaves of Grass* (Philadelphia: David Mackay, 1891), p. 207.
21  Whitman, *Leaves of Grass*, p. 321.
22  Whitman, *Leaves of Grass*, p. 323.
23  Ian Bradley, *The Quiet Haven: An Anthology of Readings on Death and Heaven* (London: Darton, Longman & Todd, 2021), pp. 124, 126.
24  John Baillie, *Diary of Private Prayer* (New York: Scribner, 2014), p. 9.
25  Joanne Coyle, *Showing Us the Way Home: The Gift of Near-Death Experiences* (Dundee: Joanne Coyle, 2019), pp. 34–5.
26  Matheson, *Moments on the Mount*, pp. 182–3.
27  George Matheson, *Rests by the River* (New York: A. C. Armstrong, 1906), pp. 27–8.

[28] George Matheson, *Thoughts for Life's Journey* (London: Hodder, 1908), pp. 251–2.
[29] Robert Bickersteth, *Recognition of Friends in Heaven* (London: J. Nisbet, 1866), pp. 42–7.
[30] George Matheson, *Messages of Hope* (London: Hodder & Stoughton, 1908), pp. 196–7.
[31] Matheson, *Moments on the Mount*, p. 32.
[32] George Matheson, *Searchings in the Silence* (London: Cassell, 1895), pp. 210–12.

8

# "A grand mysterious harmony floods me"

*John Henry Newman*

John Henry Newman (1801–90) was second only to Alfred Tennyson in the nineteenth century in terms of the impact of his writings on death and what follows it. Especially influential was his lengthy poem *The Dream of Gerontius*, published in 1865. Michael Wheeler puts it thus: "After *In Memoriam*, Newman's *The Dream of Gerontius* was the best known and most frequently discussed literary work on the subject of death and the future life to be published during the Victorian Age."[1] For Geoffrey Rowell, it "summed up much that Victorian believers wished to affirm about the future life, as can be seen by its frequent quotation by writers of all Christian denominations".[2] Among those deeply affected by *The Dream of Gerontius* was the young Edward Elgar, who was given a copy as a present on his marriage in 1889 by the parish priest of the Roman Catholic church that he attended in Worcester. It contained handwritten transcriptions of notes that had been made on the poem by General Charles Gordon, the Evangelical soldier best known for his role in the siege of Khartoum. Elgar's setting of the poem in 1900 gave it a new lease of life and added to its spiritual influence and aura.

Newman's approach was very different from Tennyson's and indeed from that of most of the other writers considered in this book. He was much less troubled by doubt, although it was not wholly absent, and much more dogmatic and certain in his approach, especially after his reception into the Roman Catholic Church in 1845. Where Tennyson based his thoughts on the possibility and nature of a future life on his imagination and feeling, "faintly trusting the larger hope", Newman stood on the clear teachings of the Church. His theological outlook was much more conservative and less liberal, encompassing an overwhelming sense of sin, and an emphasis on death bringing judgment in an individual face-to-face encounter with God. This led him to lean heavily on the Catholic doctrine of Purgatory which dominates *The Dream of Gerontius*.

There is, in fact, really very little about heaven and what it will be like in *The Dream of Gerontius*, although there are hints of his thoughts in some of Newman's other writings. His firm adherence to the Anglo-Catholic doctrine of reserve meant that he was not given to speculation on the subject, although there is one rare early excursion into imagining what it may be like in his poem "Waiting for the Morning". It was written in 1835 when he was still an Anglican and vicar of the university church in Oxford and had recently embarked on his *Tracts for the Times*, which set in train the Tractarian movement to take the Church of England back to its Catholic roots. This poem seems to anticipate those of Christina Rossetti and others in giving quite a tangible picture of a place with a strong emphasis on rest and repose:

> They are at rest:
> We may not stir the heaven of their repose
> With loud-voiced grief or passionate request,
> Or selfish plaint for those
> Who in the mountain grots in Eden lie,
> And hear the four-fold river, as it hurries by.
>
> They hear it sweep
> In distance down the dark and savage vale;
> But they at eddying pool or current deep
> Shall never more grow pale;
> They hear, and meekly muse, as fain to know
> How long untired, unspent, that giant stream shall flow.

> And soothing sounds
> Blend with the neighbouring waters as they glide;
> Posted along the haunted garden's bounds
> Angelic forms abide,
> Echoing, as words of watch, o'er lawn and grove,
> The verses of that hymn which Seraphs chant above.

This portrayal of heaven, complete with mountain grots, haunted gardens, angelic forms and seraphic choirs, is romantic, archaic and reassuring. The main focus of the poem is on the four-fold river of Paradise, mentioned in Genesis 2:10–14 in connection with the Garden of Eden, which is described as sweeping down "the dark and savage vale" and blending with neighbouring waters as they glide along. There is nothing to fear or provoke dismay in the flow of this giant stream. The effect of its sound and flow is rather to soothe and reassure.

There is a certain ambiguity as to whether the poem is about heaven itself or the period of sleep which precedes it, as is perhaps suggested by the phrase in the second line, "the heaven of their repose". Its title, "Waiting for the Morning", hints at expectation of the beatific vision, the direct perception of God enjoyed by those in heaven, which is especially emphasized in Catholic doctrine. It is this vision that the souls in Paradise are awaiting. The closing couplet of Newman's poem "Lead, kindly light", written two years earlier, which describes the arrival of morning after a long, dark night, can possibly be taken as another reference to the heavenly state and what awaits us there:

> And with the morn those angel faces smile,
> Which I have loved long since, and lost a while.

That is certainly how it was interpreted in a sonnet written after the death of Catharine Tait and based on "Lead, kindly light". Its anonymous author portrayed her as dwelling in heaven:

> Where in the light of everlasting day,
> Lost 'angel-faces' wait her near the Throne.[3]

"Waiting for the Morning" is a rare exercise in imagination by Newman as to the nature of heaven. He was generally more circumspect and reserved in writing about it, although he did make clear his belief that it is "not like this world" but much more like a church, "because both in the one and the other, there is one single sovereign subject—religion—brought before us".[4] His view of heaven was theocentric rather than anthropocentric, with a focus on the worship of and closeness to God. He echoed F. D. Maurice in insisting that the concept of eternity was not to be understood in temporal terms:

> It is not infinite time. Time implies a process—it involves the connexion and action of one portion of time upon another—if eternity be an eternal *now*, eternal punishment is the fact that a person *is* in suffering; he suffers today and tomorrow and so on for ever—but not in a continuation—all is complete in every time, —there is no memory, no anticipation, no growth of intensity from succession.[5]

It is significant that, in stark contrast to Maurice, Matheson and other liberally inclined Broad Church Protestant clerics, Newman's thoughts on eternity were focused on punishment. He never lost the belief instilled into him in his Evangelical upbringing, which was Calvinistic rather than Arminian, in the reality of hell and of everlasting punishment. In his famous *Apologia Pro Vita Sua* (1864), he affirmed his strong belief in "the doctrine of eternal punishment, as delivered by Our Lord himself, in as true a sense as that of eternal happiness".[6] Indeed, he took this doctrine to be "the turning point between Christianity and pantheism, the critical doctrine, the very characteristic of Christianity".[7]

Unsurprisingly, given his background and beliefs, Newman had an overwhelming sense of sin, a horror of judgment and of meeting God face to face, three themes which figure prominently in *The Dream of Gerontius*. He was preoccupied with the question "What must I do to be saved?" and with the need for both repentance and sanctification. This crystallized around his conviction that holiness is the pre-eminent qualification for heaven. An unholy man cannot bear to see the face of God. Echoing Matheson, he maintained that "heaven is *not* heaven, is not a place of happiness, except to the holy"—for "an irreligious man" it would be nothing less than hell.⁸

This abiding concern with the continuing reality of sin, present even in those who are baptized and have been regular churchgoers leading blameless lives, and with the need to purge it explains Newman's enthusiastic embrace of the doctrine of Purgatory, a post-mortem period of penal purification, of which he is one of the prime exponents in the nineteenth century. For him, salvation is not easily won and is no done deal at death, when the road to hell stretches out as a real and present possibility. He gives a much grimmer and more terrifying picture of the immediate aftermath of death than most of his contemporaries quoted in this book:

> There will be no need of shutting your eyes to this world, when this world has vanished from you, and you have nothing before you but the throne of God and the slow continual movements about it in preparation of the judgement. In that interval, when you are in that vast receptacle of disembodied souls, what will be your thoughts about the world which you have left! How poor will seem its aims, how faint, its keenest pleasures, compared with the eternal aims, the infinite pleasures.⁹

*The Dream of Gerontius* is largely set in this period of "slow continual movements" around the throne of God in preparation for judgment within "that vast receptacle of disembodied souls". It recounts the experience of someone going through death and the judgment that follows it. Gerontius is conceived as Everyman, a Christian believer who has led a good but not exceptional life. Newman wrote it 20 years after being received into the Roman Catholic Church at a time when he was seized with a sense of his own mortality, possibly as a result of the stroke suffered by his good friend John Keble.

Much of the first part of the poem is made up of quotations of sections of the Roman rite for the Commendation of the Soul. A key moment comes at the beginning of the second part when Gerontius has just died, having been sent on his way out of the world by the prayer of commendation offered at his death bed by the priest, whose ever-more distant voice he hears as in a dream. His soul describes feeling an inexpressive lightness and sense of freedom, along with a silence and deep rest which has something of sternness and pain as well as being soothing and sweet. This does not seem to be the long sleep that follows death but rather a more transitory and brief state between life and death, as suggested by the fact that the voice of the priest and friends gathered around his bedside can still be heard, albeit ever fainter. But what is striking is that he hears "no more the busy beat of time" and seems rather to enter an eternal present where one moment does not differ from the rest, reminiscent of John Donne's "one equal eternity":

> I went to sleep; and now I am refreshed.
> A strange refreshment for I feel in me
> An inexpressive lightness, and a sense
> Of freedom, as I were at length myself,
> And ne'er had been before. How still it is!
> I hear no more the busy beat of time,
> No, nor my fluttering breath, nor struggling pulse;
> Nor does one moment differ from the next.
>
> I had a dream; yes—some one softly said
> 'He's gone'; and then a sigh went round the room.
> And then I surely heard a priestly voice
> Cry *'Subvenite'*; and they knelt in prayer.
> I seem to hear him still; but thin and low,
> And fainter and more faint the accents come,
> As at an ever-widening interval.
> Ah! whence is this? What is this severance?
>
> This silence pours a solitariness
> Into the very essence of my soul:
> And the deep rest so soothing and so sweet
> Hath something too of sternness and of pain . . .

Gerontius asks himself if he is alive or dead and concludes that he is "in the body still":

> So much I know, not knowing how I know,
> That the vast universe, where I have dwelt,
> Is quitting me, or I am quitting it . . .

This is followed by a sense that he is being carried and moved forward by the first of the many angels who make an appearance in the poem:

> Another marvel: some one has me fast
> Within his ample palm; 'tis not a grasp
> Such as they use on earth, but all around
> Over the surface of my subtle being,
> As though I were a sphere, and capable
> To be accosted thus, a uniform
> And gentle pressure tells me I am not
> Self-moving, but borne forward on my way.
> And hark! I hear a singing; yet in sooth
> I cannot of that music rightly say
> Whether I hear, or touch, or taste the tones.
> Oh, what a heart-subduing melody!

Gerontius' soul is led by the angel who greets him on the other side to the judgment court where he is assailed by a chorus of demons seeking to gather souls for hell. The Angel of Agony pleads his cause, invoking the double agony undergone by Christ in the garden of Gethsemane and on the cross of Calvary, and he is also helped through the ordeal of judgment by the prayers of the priest and the friends whose voices he hears again. His soul begs to go down into Purgatory:

> Take me away, and in the lowest deep
> There let me be,
> And there in hope the lone night-watches keep,
> Told out for me.
> There, motionless and happy in my pain,
> Lone, not forlorn,—
> There will I sing my sad perpetual strain,
> Until the morn.

> There will I sing, and soothe my stricken breast,
> Which ne'er can cease
> To throb, and pine, and languish, till possest
> Of its Sole Peace.
> There will I sing my absent Lord and Love:—
> Take me away,
> That sooner I may rise, and go above,
> And see Him in the truth of everlasting day.

Gerontius' prayer is answered. His ransomed soul is lowered into the "penal waters" of Purgatory, enfolded in the loving arms of another angel, who promises that yet more angels will tend and nurse him. Angels play a particularly prominent role in Newman's eschatology. As we have already seen, "angelic forms" feature in "Waiting for the Morning" and "angel faces" in "Lead, kindly light". *The Dream of Gerontius* is full of them. As Michael Wheeler comments, "Among the great divines of the nineteenth century, Newman had the strongest sense of the ministry of angels."[10] The particular angel assigned to look after Gerontius in his journey to the next world leaves him with these words:

> Softly and gently, dearly-ransomed soul,
> In my most loving arms I now enfold thee,
> And, o'er the penal waters, as they roll,
> I poise thee, and I lower thee, and hold thee.
>
> And carefully I dip thee in the lake,
> And thou, without a sob or a resistance,
> Dost through the flood thy rapid passage take,
> Sinking deep, deeper into the dim distance.
>
> Angels, to whom the willing task is given,
> Shall tend, and nurse, and lull thee, as thou liest;
> And Masses on the earth, and prayers in heaven,
> Shall aid thee at the Throne of the Most Highest.

> Farewell, but not for ever! brother dear,
> Be brave and patient on thy bed of sorrow;
> Swiftly shall pass thy night of trial here,
> And I will come and wake thee on the morrow.

So it is that the poem ends not in heaven but rather in the penal waters of Purgatory, so different from Matheson's ocean of God's love. It is on the "bed of sorrow" and in the "night of trial" that Newman leaves the soul of Gerontius, albeit with the angel's promise that the latter will pass quickly and that, as in "Lead, kindly light", a morning of awakening will soon come.

*The Dream of Gerontius* has more to say about the immediate post-mortem state and about the intermediate state of Purgatory than it does about heaven. It is much darker and more frightening than most of the other Victorian sources discussed in this book in its focus on judgment and emphasis on the terrifying reality of hell. However, it also shares in several of the characteristic Victorian imaginings of what follows after death, not least in the prominent role given to angels, as messengers, advocates and bearers of the soul to God, with a ministry similar to that of priests in this world in facilitating the passage of souls to heaven. There is also the familiar emphasis on the suspension and compression of time in the eternal now and a clear depiction of heaven as first and foremost a place of continual worship of God, as expressed by the repeated chorus from the choir of angels, "Praise to the holiest in the height", which has become the most enduring and well-known part of Newman's poem. The muted singing of this hymn by the "choir of angelicals", marked *ppp* or *pianississimo* in the score, at the very end of Edward Elgar's sublime setting of *The Dream of Gerontius*, does provide a final affirmative and lingering intimation of heaven, even if it is not there in the original poem.

*The Dream of Gerontius* was widely read in the last three decades of the nineteenth century before Elgar set it to music in 1900. Understandably it had a particular appeal to Roman Catholics and High Anglicans, by whom it was much quoted and cited in support of the doctrine of Purgatory, both for portraying its purifying and penalizing character, and emphasizing its importance in the immediate post-mortem state as a necessary prelude to ascent to heaven and the beatific vision. Prominent among the Anglican advocates of Purgatory was Herbert Luckock (see p. 101). In two important and influential works, *After Death* (1879) and *The Intermediate State* (1890), he emphasized the need for a purification after death. Geoffrey Rowell points out that espousal of a doctrine of Purgatory brought several Tractarians in the later nineteenth century close to universalism: "If a man was allowed an 'adequate probation' after death, was it conceivable that any in the end should reject God?"[11] They were encouraged in this view by the strong universalist tradition in the early church, particularly in the writings of the Greek Fathers.

Among Newman's Roman Catholic contemporaries there were some, like Father Joseph Furniss, who went even further than him in emphasizing the terrifying reality of the everlasting fires of hell (see p. 93), and others who were more inclined to emphasize God's mercy and love and to make rather less of the awful fear of judgment after death that looms so large in *The Dream of Gerontius*. Pre-eminent in this latter group was Frederick William Faber, who followed his friend and mentor Newman into the Roman Catholic Church in 1845. Faber's hymn "Come to Jesus", which emphasizes the wideness of God's mercy, has already been quoted (p. 87). In his 1857 book *The Creator and the Creature*, Faber reversed the conclusion of Furniss and many Evangelicals that the majority of people, including many who regarded themselves as Christians, would be damned. He argued rather that the vast majority of humankind would be saved and go to heaven, resting his case on the purifying effects of Purgatory and the overwhelming mercy of God:

> God is infinitely merciful to every soul ... and, as to those who may be lost, I confidently believe that our Heavenly Father threw His arms around each created spirit, and looked it full in the face with the bright eyes of love, in the deliberate darkness of its mortal life.[12]

Newman was much taken by Faber's poem "The Eternal Years", with its affirmation that

death will have rainbows round it, seen
Through calm contrition's tears,
If tranquil hope but trims her lamp
At the Eternal Years.

He asked to have it sung to him in his final illness, remarking that "'Lead, Kindly Light' are the words of one seeking the truth. 'The Eternal Years' are those of one who has found it."[13]

Frederick Faber was undoubtedly closer to the *zeitgeist* of the age in his positive embrace of death, his universalist tendencies and his emphasis on God's love and mercy than was John Henry Newman, with his focus on the terrifying nature of judgment and the ever-present danger of descending into hell. The entire text of "The Eternal Years" was, in fact, printed as an appendix at the end of an edition of *The Dream of Gerontius* published not long after Newman's death, at the request of its editor, Maurice Egan, Professor of English Language and Literature in the Catholic University of America, Washington, D.C. This was presumably done, like Elgar's reprise of "Praise to the holiest in the height", to give it a rather calmer and more positive conclusion and make it altogether more Victorian.[14]

# Notes

1. Michael Wheeler, *Death and the Future Life in Victorian Literature and Theology* (Cambridge: Cambridge University Press, 1990), p. 305.
2. Geoffrey Rowell, *Hell and the Victorians: A Study of the Nineteenth-century Theological Controversies concerning Eternal Punishment and the Future Life* (Oxford: Clarendon Press, 1974), p. 160.
3. William Benham, *Catharine and Crauford Tait: A Memoir* (London: Macmillan, 1879), p. 390.
4. John Henry Newman, *Parochial and Plain Sermons* (London: Rivingtons, 1868), I, 5.
5. Wilfrid Ward, *The Life of John Henry Cardinal Newman* (London: Longmans, Green, 1912), I, 246.
6. Rowell, *Hell and the Victorians*, p. 92.
7. Rowell, *Hell and the Victorians*, p. 163.
8. Newman, *Parochial and Plain Sermons*, I, 7.
9. Newman, *Parochial and Plain Sermons*, IV, 92.
10. Wheeler, *Death and the Future Life*, p. 135.
11. Rowell, *Hell and the Victorians*, p. 107.
12. Frederick William Faber, *The Creator and the Creature: or The Wonders of Divine Love* (London: Thomas Richardson & Son, 1858), p. 393.
13. Mountstuart Elphinstone Grant Duff, *Notes from a Diary, 1889-1891* (London: John Murray, 1901), I, 72.
14. John Henry Newman, *The Dream of Gerontius* (London: Longmans, Green, 1903).

9

# "The caterpillar dies into the butterfly"

*Charles Kingsley, Frederick Robertson, John Clare, Walt Whitman, Mary Bradley and Ellice Hopkins*

This chapter explores the views of some of the many nineteenth-century preachers and poets who thought about human death and what followed it by drawing analogies from the processes of biological and physical decay and renewal in the natural world. They were strongly influenced by the theory of evolution and by a kenotic theology of sacrifice and often cited both the image in the Book of Revelation of the lamb slain from the foundation of the world and Jesus' words as recorded in John's Gospel about the need for a grain of wheat to fall into the ground and die if it was to produce fruit. For them, death was both natural and benign, being an essential precondition for new life and as such to be regarded as a beginning rather than an end. Most of those who espoused this view were liberal Broad Church Christians who found themselves in conflict with Evangelicals' insistence on death as the wages of sin, and as such something fundamentally evil, unfortunate and unplanned. While they were less focused on heaven than those featured in previous chapters, and in some cases uncertain and even uneasy about it, they find a place in this book because of their strong sense of there being something positive following and coming out of death, even if it is just making space for others and creating the conditions for new life. Some gave poetic and artistic expression to this belief by celebrating the flowers that grew out of the rich soil in the graveyards in which most of the Victorian dead reposed. Others took the cycle of nature as a pointer to resurrection and saw the caterpillar's transition into a butterfly as a metaphor for the transformation described by Paul when he wrote about the mortal nature putting on immortality in his first letter to the Corinthians.

An early Victorian devotee of what might be called this theology of recycling was the fiercely anti-Catholic Anglican clergyman, Christian Socialist and author, Charles Kingsley, best remembered today for his novel *The Water Babies*. He expresses its essence very simply in his poem "Easter Week", which likens Christ's resurrection to the new life that bursts forth from the ground in spring in a simile which anticipates John Macleod Campbell Crum's early-twentieth-century hymn "Now the green blade riseth from the buried earth":

> See the land, her Easter keeping,
> Rises as her Maker rose.
> Seeds, so long in darkness sleeping,
> Burst at last from winter snows.[1]

While its focus is on the resurrection of Christ rather than on human resurrection or immortality, Kingsley's poem continues with the line, "Earth with heaven above rejoices", providing an acknowledgement of the realm where souls will go, although, as we will see, the author was distinctly uneasy about the envisaging of heaven by many of his contemporaries as a distinct place in the sky.

Kingsley draws much more dramatically and extensively on the natural world to show the centrality of self-sacrifice and the principle of life coming out of death in his first published work, the dramatic poem *The Saint's Tragedy* (1848), where he puts these words into the mouth of St Elizabeth of Hungary:

> Nought lives for self—All, all—from crown to footstool—
> The Lamb, before the world's foundations slain—
> The angels, ministers to God's elect—
> The sun, who only shines to light a world—
> The clouds, whose glory is to die in showers—
> The fleeting streams, who in their ocean-graves
> Flee the decay of stagnant self-content—
> The oak, ennobled by the shipwright's axe—

> The soil, which yields its marrow to the flower—
> The flower, which feeds a thousand velvet worms,
> Born only to be prey for every bird—
> All spend themselves for others: and shall man,
> Earth's rosy blossom—image of his God—
> Whose twofold being is the mystic knot
> Which couples earth and heaven—doubly bound
> As being both worm and angel, to that service
> By which both worms and angels hold their life—
> Shall he, whose every breath is debt on debt,
> Refuse, without some hope of further wage
> Which he calls Heaven, to be what God has made him?
> No! let him show himself the creature's lord
> By freewill gift of that self-sacrifice
> Which they perforce by nature's law must suffer.

The description here of humans as both worms and angels, bound in the mystic knot which joins earth and heaven, is striking, as is the clear suggestion that their actions should be motivated by a voluntary spirit of self-sacrifice rather than any thought of that wage or reward known as heaven. This point is reiterated at the end of Elizabeth's speech when she asks God:

> Oh, thrust me forth,
> Forth, Lord, from self, until I toil and die
> No more for Heaven and bliss, but duty, Lord,
> Duty to Thee, although my meed should be
> The hell which I deserve![2]

As these last lines show, Kingsley is not over enamoured with the widespread Victorian idea of heavenly bliss as a reward for the toils and labours of life. For him, the stern call of duty and self-sacrifice rather than the thought of eternal reward should be the animating principle for Christians. In a sermon preached in Eversley, Hampshire, where he was vicar, and published in 1849, he attacks the common misconception that heaven is a place up in the sky to which people fly away when they die:

> We are in heaven now—if we had but faith to see it. Oh, get rid of those carnal, heathen notions about heaven, which tempt men to fancy that, after having misused this place—God's earth—for a whole life, they are to fly away when they die, like swallows in autumn, to another place—they know not where—where they are to be very happy—they know not why or how, nor do I know either. Heaven is not a mere PLACE, my friends. All places are heaven, if you will be heavenly in them. Heaven is where God is and Christ is. And hell is where God is not and Christ is not. The Bible says, no doubt, there is a place now—somewhere beyond the skies—where Christ especially shews forth His glory—a heaven of heavens: and for reasons which I cannot explain, there must be such a place. But, at all events, here is heaven; for Christ is here and God is here, if we will open our eyes and see them.[3]

Kingsley's view that heaven is a state of being rather than a place, and one which can be experienced in this life, closely echoes the thoughts of F. D. Maurice. It was no accident that *The Saint's Tragedy* had a preface by Maurice, who was Kingsley's close friend and mentor, and it is highly appropriate that the busts of the two men stand side by side in Poets' Corner in Westminster Abbey. They shared an overwhelming sense of the power of sacrifice, and in particular of self-sacrifice, which they took to be both at the heart of the very being of God and also the animating principle of the universe, as shown in the workings of evolution and the cycles of nature. They expressed this in theological terms in what is technically known as the doctrine of kenosis, or self-emptying, which is particularly associated with the description in Philippians 2:5–9 of Christ Jesus humbling himself and taking the nature of a servant. Jesus' voluntary self-surrender and humiliation was seen both as revelatory of the essential character of God and as normative for human behaviour. Christ's sacrifice and death on the cross, followed by his direct descent into hell and his resurrection, drew his body, understood not just as the Church or Christians but potentially as all humanity and indeed all creation, into participation in a paradigm of life through death whereby the earthly body was transformed into a new heavenly one as Paul indicated in 1 Corinthians 15.[4]

This kenotic Christology was central to the thinking of several of the leading Victorian Broad Church liberal theologians. Maurice wrote of sacrifice being quite simply "the doctrine of the Bible, the doctrine of the Gospel. The Bible is, from first to last, setting forth to us the meaning of Sacrifice."[5] George Matheson took a similar view, as expounded in his poem entitled "The Divine Plan of Creation" inspired by the text "The Lamb slain from the foundation of the world" in Revelation 13:8:

> Thou hast, O Lord, a wondrous plan,
> To build a tower to reach the skies;
> Its base is earth, its progress man,
> Its summit sacrifice.[6]

This emphasis on sacrifice led to a strong attachment to the social gospel and concern with this world rather than the next. It was no coincidence that the leading exponents of kenosis were Christian Socialists actively concerned with fighting inequality and injustice here and now on earth and dismissive of popular pie-in-the-sky preaching which counselled the poor to accept their lot in life and wait for their rewards in heaven. But their focus on the coming of God's kingdom on earth in what is technically called realized eschatology, their strong belief in the centrality of sacrifice and surrender, and their conviction, reinforced by their observation of the cycles of nature, that death was a necessary precursor to life, also gave them an interest in the idea and the reality of resurrection, both as experienced by Christ and as the means by which Christians would attain everlasting life.

Among the most influential and persuasive exponents of this theology in the mid-nineteenth century was the Broad Church Anglican clergyman Frederick William Robertson, whose sermons preached during his time as incumbent of the fashionable Trinity Chapel, Brighton between 1847 and 1853 were hugely popular and became bestsellers in their published form. For Robertson, "sacrifice, conscious and unconscious, for the life of others" is "the grand law of the universe". In a sermon preached in 1849, he declared that "it is a mysterious and fearful thing to observe how all God's universe is built upon this law, how it penetrates and pervades all Nature, so that if it were to cease, Nature would cease to exist."[7]

In this same sermon Robertson makes much of Jesus' words about the necessity of the corn of wheat falling into the ground and dying. He interprets them as pointing to sacrificial death as the basis of the evolution of all life:

> The mountain rock must have its surface rusted into putrescence and become dead soil before the herb can grow. The destruction of the mineral is the life of the vegetable. Again the same process begins. The 'corn of wheat' dies, and out of death more abundant life is born. Out of the soil in which deciduous leaves are buried, the young tree shoots vigorously, and strikes its roots deep down into the realm of decay and death. Upon the life of the vegetable world, the myriad forms of higher life sustain themselves—still the same law: the sacrifice of life to give life.[8]

He goes on to suggest that the same principle of life coming out of death applied in the animal kingdom and among humans. In another sermon preached in 1850 on the sacrifice of Christ, he interprets the cross as revelatory of the internal character of God in a way that to some extent anticipates the argument of Jürgen Moltmann's *The Crucified God* more than a century later:

> The death of Christ was a representation of the life of God. To me this is the profoundest of all truths, that the whole of the life of God is the sacrifice of self ... Creation itself is sacrifice—the self-impartation of the divine being. Redemption, too, is sacrifice. Else it could not be love; for which reason we will not surrender one iota of the truth that the death of Christ was the sacrifice of God—the manifestation once in time of that which is the eternal law of His life.

Thus understood, the cross is not just the supreme example of the principle of sacrifice that is "the grand law of the universe" but also the key and means to the fulfilment of human destiny: "If man is to rise into the life of God, he must be absorbed into the spirit of that sacrifice—he must die with Christ if he would enter into his proper life." Drawing strongly on St Paul's words in 2 Corinthians 5:14–15, Robertson describes the power of the cross in terms of radical inclusivity and participation:

> The influence of that sacrifice on man is the introduction of the principle of self-sacrifice into his nature ... not He died that we might not die, but that in His death we might be dead, and that in His sacrifice we might become each a sacrifice to God. Moreover His death is identical with life. They who are called dead are 'they who live'... Death, therefore—that is the sacrifice of self—is equivalent to life.[9]

Although the strength of these beliefs gave Robertson an essentially positive view of death as the gateway to life, he did not minimize its terrors and the fear surrounding it. In a sermon on "Victory Over Death" preached in 1852, he acknowledges and probes the reason for what he describes as "the awfulness which hangs round the dying hour":

> Let us search why it is we shrink from death. This reason, brethren, we shall find, that it presents to us the idea of not being. Talk as we will of immortality, there is an obstinate feeling that we cannot master, that we end in death; and that may be felt together with the firmest belief of a resurrection. Brethren, our faith tells us one thing, and our sensations tell us another. When we die, we are surrendering in truth all that with which we have associated existence. All that we know of life is connected with a shape, a form, a body of materialism; and now that that is palpably melting away into nothingness, the boldest heart may be excused a shudder, when there is forced upon it, in spite of itself, the idea of ceasing forever.[10]

So Robertson's embrace of death was not undertaken lightly, and he retained a clear pastoral appreciation of its pain and apparent finality. Ultimately, however, he put his faith in the power of sacrifice and the hope of human resurrection from the dead, as promised and signalled through the resurrection of Christ. Meanwhile, the call to Christians in this life is crystal clear: "To gain mastery over self, and sin, and doubt, and fear: till the last coldness, coming across the brow, tells us that all is over and our warfare accomplished—that we are safe, the everlasting arms beneath us—that is our calling."[11]

Other Victorian divines shared the view that the motif of life rising out of death in the natural world is both analogous to and illustrative of the Christian doctrine of resurrection to eternal life. It is clearly stated by James Buchanan, a minister in the Free Church of Scotland and Professor of Systematic Theology at New College, Edinburgh, in a treatise published in 1864 and entitled *Analogy*: "The future resurrection of the body has its natural analogue in the annual resurrection of nature from the death-like torpor of winter."[12] It was a theme also taken up by poets, notably by John Clare, the farm labourer's son and devout Anglican known as the "Northamptonshire peasant poet", in "All Nature has a feeling", written in 1845:

> All nature has a feeling: woods, fields, brooks
> Are life eternal; and in silence they
> Speak happiness beyond the reach of books;
> There's nothing mortal in them; their decay
> Is the green life of change; to pass away
> And come again in blooms revivified.
> Its birth was heaven, eternal is its stay,
> And with the sun and moon shall still abide
> Beneath their day and night and heaven wide.[13]

For Clare, the circle of life in the natural world is divinely ordained, with its birth in heaven, and speaks clearly of resurrection and eternal life. Other nineteenth-century poets equally fascinated by the process of recycling in nature took a less explicitly Christian and theological approach while still marvelling at the way life comes out of death. Perhaps the most famous and powerful poetic treatment of this theme is "This Compost", written in 1856 by the American poet Walt Whitman. It asks how vibrant new life constantly comes out of the earth that is so full of the decay and putrescence of rotting corpses:

O how can it be that the ground itself does not sicken?
How can you be alive, you growths of spring?
How can you furnish health, you blood of herbs,
roots, orchards, grain?
Are they not continually putting distemper'd corpses
in you?
Is not every continent work'd over and over with sour
dead?

. . .

Behold this compost! behold it well!
Perhaps every mite has once form'd part of a sick
person—Yet behold!
The grass covers the prairies,
The bean bursts noiselessly through the mould in the
garden,
The delicate spear of the onion pierces upward,
The apple-buds cluster together on the apple-branches,
The resurrection of the wheat appears with pale visage
out of its graves,
The tinge awakes over the willow-tree and the mulberry-tree,
The he-birds carol mornings and evenings, while the
she-birds sit on their nests,
The young of poultry break through the hatch'd eggs,
The new-born of animals appear—the calf is dropt
from the cow, the colt from the mare,
Out of its little hill faithfully rise the potato's dark
green leaves,
Out of its hill rises the yellow maize-stalk;
The summer growth is innocent and disdainful above
all those strata of sour dead.[14]

Whitman goes on to say that he is terrified of the earth because of the calm and patient way in which "it grows such sweet things out of such corruptions ... distills such exquisite winds out of such infused fetor ... gives such divine materials to men, and accepts such leavings from them at last". He is in awe of this process which turns diseased corpses into "sumptuous crops". It gives him an essentially positive view of death as the necessary fuel for new life. He takes this theme further in his 1859 poem "The Cradle Endlessly Rocking" about a boy on a beach witnessing the death of a bird and the effect it has on its mate. The boy asks nature to give him a word "superior to all" and the sea responds by repeatedly but plainly whispering to him "the low and delicious word death". This leads to a realization that death is indeed the source of the poet's muse. For many critics, Whitman's positive embrace of it in these two poems typifies what has been called the Bright Romantic approach to death in the mid-nineteenth century.

In Victorian Britain, the idea that death provides the necessary raw materials for life in the form of compost and loam was often focused on the churchyards and cemeteries in which the great majority of the population were buried. Known as "God's acres", they were revered and celebrated as the places not just where the dead slept, but also where their decomposing bodies provided the nutrition for plants, especially flowers, to grow. The grave was seen as a flower bed as well as a bed in which the sleeping soul lay, its earth protecting and nourishing the dead seed from which new life would spring. Elizabeth Stone devoted a whole chapter to "Flowers on Graves" in her popular book *God's Acre* (1858). Describing graveyards as gardens which to some extent realize and represent the landscape of heaven here on earth, she points out that "the word 'Paradise' literally signifies a garden and that it was in a garden that Christ was laid to rest and resurrected". She commends flowers as "emblems of resurrection" and evergreens as "a type of immortality" as particularly appropriate for planting in churchyards and cemeteries.[15]

This was a popular theme for poets. We have already noted the prominence of the imagery of flowers growing over the bodies lying in graves in Christina Rossetti's poems (pp. 74–5). It is there, too, in Tennyson's *In Memoriam*:

> Tis well; 'tis something; we may stand
> Where he in English earth is laid,
> And from his ashes may be made
> The violet of his native land.

In his poem "Graves of Infants", John Clare gives the flowers that grow over infants' graves a double meaning—at one level they are mourners, weeping over those below, while at another they are representations of the closing of their lives and the repose of their spirits:

> Infants' gravemounds are steps of angels, where
> Earth's brightest gems of innocence repose.
> God is their parent, so they need no tear;
>
> He takes them to his bosom from earth's woes,
> A bud their lifetime and a flower their close.
> Their spirits are the Iris of the skies,
> Needing no prayers; a sunset's happy close.
> Gone are the bright rays of their soft blue eyes;
> Flowers weep in dew-drops o'er them, and the gale gently sighs.[16]

In another of his poems, Clare compares the happy state of the soul of an infant who has died before it knew how to sin to the smiling flowers that grow over its grave:

> Beneath the sod where smiling creep
> The daisies into view,
> The ashes of an Infant sleep,
> Whose soul's as smiling too;
> Ah! doubly happy, doubly blest,
> (Had I so happy been!)
> Recall'd to heaven's eternal rest,
> Ere it knew how to sin.[17]

William Walsham How, the moderate Tractarian Anglican clergyman who became the first Bishop of Wakefield and was a keen amateur botanist and naturalist, uses the imagery of flowers growing over a child's grave to make a somewhat different theological point in a poem he wrote in 1847 while a curate at Kidderminster entitled "Funeral of a child in Spring". It ends with an injunction to the "little mourners" standing in sadness around the grave to plant seeds in its "chilly earth" and so model the resurrection:

> Children! Watch the verdure shine,
> And with quiet gladness twine
> Wreaths of flowers for a sign.
>
> Plant upon the rounded clay
> Plants that shall be blooming gay,
> Every year upon this day.
>
> For the seed, that now ye sow
> In the chilly earth below,
> Shall a glorious flower blow:—
>
> 'Sown in weakness, raised in power',
> In the eternal Springtide's bower
> It shall bloom, a glorious flower![18]

Michael Wheeler has pointed to the number of Victorian paintings of graveyards which illustrate the theme of life coming out of death. The best-known and most powerful is almost certainly *The Doubt: Can those dry bones live?*, painted by Henry Bowler in 1855 as a meditation on Tennyson's *In Memoriam* It shows a young woman in mourning leaning over a gravestone on which are carved the name "John Faithful" and the biblical text "I am the Resurrection and the Life". In front of it is an open grave with a skull and bones protruding from the earth. A yellow butterfly sits on the skull. Next to the grave a germinating chestnut sits on a stone set flat in the ground and carved with the word *"Resurgam"* ("I shall rise again") and behind it a large, spreading chestnut tree overarches the entire scene with its distinctive foliage. Two more butterflies fly in front of other gravestones. The painting's title and the expression on the young woman's face both suggest doubt about eternal life, but the butterflies, the chestnut on the stone and the mighty tree that has grown from a similar one in the ground act as signs of resurrection. In Wheeler's words:

> Bowler's *The Doubt* confronts the reality of physical decay, and the exhumed bones exposed to public view remind us of the radical opposition between the deep grave below ground (corruption, darkness and death) and the gravestone inscription above ground (incorruption, light and new life). The mysterious transformation of the small chestnut into the tree, the dimensions of which can only be guessed at, is an adequate if limited analogy for the mysterious transformation that is the resurrection of the body ... The stark reality of the exhumed bones is not erased, or explained away, but rather held in tension with the hope of resurrection offered by the text from John 11 on the gravestone. Thus the viewer is driven back to the ultimate question of faith which confronts the mourner.[19]

While Wheeler dwells especially on the significance of the chestnut in this painting, it is its other striking visual image of resurrection, the butterfly, which is more often used by the Victorians as a pointer to the reality of heaven and life beyond death. There is, of course, a long Christian tradition of the butterfly representing the soul and what happens to it after death. The Victorians, with their strong interest in entomology, were particularly enthusiastic about taking the death of the caterpillar, with its cells breaking down and then reforming to emerge from the chrysalis as a wholly new species, as indicative and illustrative of the transformation of human bodies at the resurrection as described by Paul in 1 Corinthians 15.

One of the first to draw this analogy was Richard Whately, Archbishop of Dublin from 1831 to 1863. Noting that the Greek word "psyche" can be translated as both "soul" and "butterfly", he observed that "when the life of the insect, in this its first stage, is to close, it becomes what is called a Pupa, enclosed in a chrysalis or cocoon and lies torpid for a time within this natural coffin, from which it issues, at the proper period, as a perfect butterfly."[20] He went on to suggest that something very similar happens to humans after death. William Walsham How is said to have written a hymn in his youth comparing the butterfly's life cycle to the resurrection, but I have not been able to find it in his collected works.[21] George MacDonald, the Scottish Congregationalist minister and author, wrote in his 1863 novel *David Elginbrod*: "I think of death as the first pulse of a new strength shaking itself free from the old mouldy remnant of earth garments, that it may begin in freedom the new life that grows out of the old period. The caterpillar dies into the butterfly."[22]

Perhaps the fullest and most dramatic exposition of this analogy was made by Margaret Gatty, a popular children's author with a particular interest in marine biology, who lived in Ecclesfield, near Sheffield, where her husband was vicar. The short story "Not Lost, but Gone Before" in her 1855 book *Parables from Nature* recounts a conversation between a caterpillar grub and a frog about whether there is any life beyond the pond where they both live. The grub is captivated when the frog tells him:

> I beheld one of your race slowly and gradually climbing, till he had left the water behind him, and was clinging firmly to his chosen support, exposed to the full glare of the sun. Rather wondering at such a sight, considering the fondness you all of you show for the shady bottom of the pond, I continued to gaze, and observed presently,—but I cannot tell you in what way the thing happened,—that a rent seemed to come in your friend's body, and by degrees, gradually and after many struggles, there emerged from it one of those radiant creatures who float through the air I spoke to you of, and dazzle the eyes of all who catch glimpses of them as they pass,—a glorious Dragon-fly!
>
> As if scarcely awakened from some perplexing dream, he lifted his wings out of the carcase he was forsaking; and though shrivelled and damp at first, they stretched and expanded in the sunshine, till they glistened as if with fire.

The grub looks for some verification of this and longs that one of these dragonflies will return to tell him and his fellow grubs of the new home that awaits them. But none ever returns despite promises from those grubs who feel themselves near death. One in particular, who feels that an invisible power is driving him upwards, promises that "on my parting words you may depend. Let the other world be what it will, gorgeous beyond all we can fancy of it, blissful beyond all we can hope of it, do not fear in me an altered or forgetful heart. If it be possible, I will return." Yet, like the others, he does not come back and leaves the other grubs left in the pond feeling fearful of death, lonely and betrayed by the one who has gone before them:

> And the Dragon-fly, meanwhile, was he really faithless, as they thought? When he burst his prison-house by the water side, and rose on glittering wings into the summer air, had he indeed no memory for the dear ones he had so lately left? No tender concern for their griefs and fears? No recollection of the promise he had made?
>
> Ah! so far from it, he thought of them amidst the transports of his wildest flights, and returned ever and ever to the precincts of that world which had once been the only world to him. But in that region also, a power was over him superior to his own, and to it his will must submit. To the world of waters he could never more return.
>
> The least touch upon its surface, as he skimmed over it with the purpose of descent, brought on a deadly shock, like that which, as a water-grub, he had experienced from emerging into air, and his wings involuntarily bore him instantly back from the unnatural contact.
>
> 'Alas! for the promise made in ignorance and presumption, miserable grub that I was,' was his bitter, constantly-repeated cry.
>
> And thus, divided and yet near, parted yet united by love, he hovered about the barrier that lay between them, never quite, perhaps, without a hope that some accident might bring his dear ones into sight.
>
> Nor was his constancy unrewarded, for as, after even his longest roamings, he never failed to return to the old spot, he was there to welcome the emancipated brother, who so soon followed him.

> And often, after that, the breezy air by the forest pond would resound in the bright summer afternoons, with the clashing of Dragon-flies' wings, as, now backwards, now forwards, now to one side, now to another, without turn or intermission, they darted over the crystal water, in the rapture of the new life.
>
> It might be, on those occasions, that some fresh arrival of kindred from below, added a keener joy to their already joyous existence. Sweet assuredly it was to each new-comer, when the riddle of his fate was solved, to find in the new region, not a strange and friendless abode, but a home rich with the welcomes of those who had gone before.
>
> Sweet also it was, and strange as sweet, to know that even while they had been trembling and fearing in their ignorant life below, gleams from the wings of those they lamented, were dropping like star-rays on their home, reflected hither and thither from the sun that shone above. Oh! if they could but have known!

At the end of this rather beautiful and moving parable, we are left with the image of hundreds of dragonflies hovering on the surface of the water, "longing to reassure the hearts of the trembling race, who are still hoping and fearing below".[23]

An even more poignant treatment of this theme is found in the poem "A Chrysalis" by the prolific American writer, Mary Emily Bradley (1835–98). It tells of a delicate little girl finding something the like of which she has never seen before. She is not sure whether it is alive or dead. Her mother tells her that it is a chrysalis and explains:

> How, slowly, in the dull brown thing
> Now still as death, a spotted wing,
> And then another, would unfold,
> Till from the empty shell would fly
> A pretty creature, by and by,
> All radiant in blue and gold.

Tragically, the girl dies before the chrysalis hatches out, leaving the grieving mother to reflect:

> Today the butterfly has flown,
> She was not here to see it fly,
> And sorrowing I wonder why
> The empty shell is mine alone.
> Perhaps the secret lies in this:
> I too had found a chrysalis,
> And Death that robbed me of delight
> Was but the radiant creature's flight![24]

The image of the chrysalis passing into the butterfly is picked up in one verse of a remarkable poem by Ellice Hopkins (1836–1904), an English social reformer who campaigned vigorously against prostitution and Victorian double standards and founded the White Cross Army to promote moral purity. Her poem "Life in Death", published in 1883 and probably written a few years earlier, sums up the widespread Victorian view that the cycle of decay and renewal found across the natural world applies also to humans and can be taken as a testament to the reality of resurrection and immortality. In it, she personifies death (in the masculine), and describes feeling him in the autumn winds, catching "his image faint and far" and hearing his "footsteps stealing by, where the long churchyard grasses sigh". But however hard she tries, and while everywhere she finds Death's hand, she never manages to encounter him face to face:

> Then I arose ere dawn, and found
> A faded lily. 'Lo, 'tis He!
> I will surprise him in his golden bed,
> Where, muffled close from light and sound,
> He sleeps the day up.' Noiselessly
> I drew the faded curtains from his head,
> And, peeping, found, not Death below,
> But fairy life set all arow.

A chrysalis next I chanced upon:
'Death in this dusty shroud has dwelt!'
But stooping saw a winged Thing, sun-kist,
Crusted with jewels Life had won
From Death's dim dust; and as I knelt
Some passion shook the jewels into mist,
Some ecstasy of coming flight,
And lo, he passed in morning light.

And as I paced, still questioning,
Behold, a dead bird at my feet;
The faded violets of his filmy eyes,
And tender loosened throat, to sing
No more to us his nocturns sweet,
Told me that death at length before me lies.
But gazing, quick I turned in fear,
Not Death, but teeming Life was there.

Then haply Death keeps house within?
And with the scalpel of keen thought
I traced the chemic travail of the brain,
The throb and pulse of Life's machine,
And mystic force with force still caught
In the embrace that maketh one of twain;
And all the beatings, swift and slow,
Of Life's vibration to and fro.

And still I found the downward swing,
Decay, but ere I cried 'Lo, here!'
The upward stroke rang out glad life and breath;
And still dead winters changed with spring,
And graves the new birth's cradle were;
And still I grasped the flying skirts of Death,
And still he turned, and beaming fair,
The radiant face of Life was there![25]

# Notes

1. Charles Kingsley, *Works*, Vol. 1 (London: Macmillan, 1884), p. 289.
2. Charles Kingsley, *The Saint's Tragedy* (London: J. W. Parker, 1848), pp. 202–3.
3. Charles Kingsley, *Twenty-five Village Sermons* (London: John W. Parker, 1849), p. 222.
4. For a fuller discussion of the kenotic theology of sacrifice developed in the latter half of the nineteenth century see the chapter "The grand law of the universe: Sacrifice in Victorian and Edwardian thought" in my book *The Power of Sacrifice* (London: Darton, Longman & Todd, 1995), pp. 161–203.
5. Frederick Denison Maurice, *The Doctrine of Sacrifice Deduced from the Scriptures* (Cambridge: Macmillan, 1854), p. xlvi.
6. George Matheson, *Sacred Songs* (Edinburgh: Blackwood, 1891), p. 13.
7. Frederick William Robertson, *Sermons, preached at Trinity Chapel, Brighton*, first series (London: Kegan Paul, 1902), p. 138.
8. Robertson, *Sermons*, first series, p. 138.
9. Frederick William Robertson, *Sermons, preached at Trinity Chapel, Brighton*, third series (London: Kegan Paul, 1902), p. 100.
10. Robertson, *Sermons*, third series, p. 184.
11. Robertson, *Sermons*, third series, p. 184.
12. James Buchanan, *Analogy* (Edinburgh: Johnstone, Hunter, 1864), p. 368.
13. *The Later Poems of John Clare*, Vol. 1, ed. E. Robinson (Oxford: Clarendon Press, 1964), p. 210.
14. *The Poems of Walt Whitman* (London: Walter Scott, 1886), pp. 237–8.
15. Elizabeth Stone, *God's Acre: Historical Notices Relating to Churchyards* (London: John W. Parker, 1858), pp. 247 and 262.
16. *Poems by John Clare* (Rugby: George Over, 1901), p. 144.
17. *Poems by John Clare*, p. 22.
18. William Walsham How, *Poems* (London: Wells, Gardner, Darton & Co., 1887), p. 23.
19. Michael Wheeler, "Can These Dry Bones Live?", in David Jasper and T. R. Wright (eds), *The Critical Spirit and the Will to Believe: Essays in Nineteenth-century Literature and Religion* (London: Macmillan, 1989), p. 30. Wheeler also discusses the painting in *Death and the Future Life in Victorian Literature and Theology* (Cambridge: Cambridge University Press, 1990), pp. 59–61.

[20] Richard Whately, *A View of Scripture Revelations Concerning a Future State* (London: Parker, 1853), p. 289.
[21] This hymn is mentioned in Bernard Braley, *Hymnwriters*, Vol. 1 (London: Stainer & Bell, 1987), p. 105.
[22] Robert Cecil, *The Masks of Death: Changing Attitudes in the Nineteenth Century* (Lewes: The Book Guild, 1991), p. 175.
[23] Mrs Alfred Gatty, *Parables from Nature* (London: Nelson, 1855), pp. 151–68.
[24] Edmund Clarence Stedman (ed.), *An American Anthology, 1787–1900* (Boston: Houghton Mifflin, 1900), p. 644.
[25] Ellice Hopkins, *Autumn Swallows: A Book of Lyrics* (London: Macmillan, 1883), pp. 1–4.

## 10

# "The heart still overrules the head"

*Poets and philosophers on the fringes of faith*

Most of those whose views on heaven have so far featured in this book were committed Christian believers, many of them ordained and some deeply devout like Christina Rossetti, Adelaide Procter and John Henry Newman. This chapter explores the views of those who were very much more on the fringes of faith, including some of the Victorian age's most noted freethinkers. They were for the most part poets and philosophers, intellectuals who were deeply affected by religious doubts and sceptical of dogma and biblical revelation. They are leading representatives of "the higher class of thinkers", who, John Ruskin noted in a letter to his father on Easter Day 1852, "for the most part have given up the peculiarly Christian doctrines, and indeed nearly all thought of a future life". Ruskin went on to say that he could not join them in this view and that "to believe in a future life is for me the only way in which I can enjoy this one".[1] In fact, many eminent Victorian freethinkers found it similarly difficult to give up all hope of a future life, however faint it might be, and they found themselves tentatively affirming the existence of heaven, albeit in a rather different form from that conceived in the popular imagination and preached by many churchmen.

Alfred Tennyson spoke for many of his fellow poets as well as for his contemporaries more generally in the way that he wrote about the possibility of an afterlife in *In Memoriam* faintly trusting the larger hope "that those we call the dead are breathers of an ampler day for ever nobler ends". His near contemporary, Robert Browning, whose own faith was precarious, confessed in a private letter in 1864 that he believed in immortality "if I have any instinct or insight,—if I can retain and rightly reason upon the rare flashes of momentary conviction that come and go in the habitual dusk and doubt of one's life".[2] Another much-read poet who clung to hope of an afterlife despite his profound religious doubts was Arthur Hugh Clough (1819–61), who is often regarded as the voice of the Victorian crisis of faith. Having resigned his Oxford fellowship because he felt that he could no longer in conscience subscribe to the teachings and articles of the Church of England, he became a leading apostle of honest doubt. In several of his poems, he seems to be clear that there is no heaven. One written in Naples on Easter Day 1849, "Christ is not risen", for example, proclaims clearly "There is no Heaven but this!" and continues:

> There is no glistening of an angel's wings,
> There is no voice of heavenly clear behest;
> let us go hence and think upon these things
> In silence which is best.[3]

Clough goes on in "Christ is not risen" to propose a hedonistic philosophy of "eat, drink and play" and a focus on this world. Characteristically, almost immediately after writing it, he penned a second Easter Day poem which proclaims that "Christ is yet risen", but it has no reference to an afterlife. In another poem probably written in 1849, however, and apparently inspired by the text in 1 Corinthians 13:12, "For now we see through a glass, darkly; but then face to face", he allows his heart to rule his head and seems enthusiastically to embrace the idea of heaven as a place where what is begun here on earth will be completed:

> Ah yet, when all is thought and said,
> The heart still overrules the head;
> Still what we hope we must believe,
> And what is given us receive.

> Must still believe, for still we hope
> That in a world of larger scope,
> What here is faithfully begun
> Will be completed, not undone.

> My child, we still must think, when we
> That ampler life together see,
> Some true result will yet appear
> Of what we are, together, here.⁴

There are striking echoes of Tennyson's *In Memoriam* in Clough's phrases "the world of larger scope" and "that ampler life". There is also a distinct pre-echo of F. D. Maurice's view that heaven will provide "scope to complete tasks which death will leave unfinished" in his couplet "What here is faithfully begun/Will be completed, not undone". His was a heaven of strenuous activity, if it did, indeed, exist, but on that last question he remained irredeemably agnostic. In his 1858 poem "O stream descending to the sea", he makes the familiar analogy between a stream running down to the sea and life descending to death. In the last two verses, he powerfully uses the imagery of the sea and its shore to express his own profound uncertainty on this matter:

> O end to which our currents tend,
> Inevitable sea,
> To which we flow, what do we know,
> What shall we guess of thee?
>
> A roar we hear upon thy shore,
> As we our course fulfil;
> Scarce we divine a sun will shine
> And be above us still.⁵

The roar that Clough hears upon the shore in this slightly bleak conclusion brings to mind the "melancholy, long, withdrawing roar" of the once full sea of faith in the poem "Dover Beach" by his contemporary Matthew Arnold. But he leaves open the possibility that the sun of eternal life and heaven will shine and that, like George Matheson, we will trace the rainbow through the rain. Meanwhile, on the other side of the Atlantic, the American Quaker poet John Greenleaf Whittier, best known to us as the author of "Dear Lord and Father of Mankind, Forgive Our Foolish Ways", was using similar imagery of the ocean and the silent shore to ponder the great unanswerable question of what lies beyond death. His 1865 poem "The Eternal Goodness", inspired by his grief at seeing friends depart, expresses a much more sure and certain hope than Clough's. He may not know the location of those islands of the blessed which have been seen as the abode of the happy dead since ancient times, but he can be in no doubt at all about God's underlying love and care. The closing lines of this poem echo John Ellerton's belief that no one dies beyond the reach of God's infinite mercy:

> I long for household voices gone,
> For vanished smiles I long,
> But God hath led my dear ones on,
> And He can do no wrong.
>
> I know not what the future hath
> Of marvel or surprise,
> Assured alone that life and death
> His mercy underlies . . .
>
> And so beside the Silent Sea
> I wait the muffled oar;
> No harm from Him can come to me
> On ocean or on shore.
>
> I know not where His islands lift
> Their fronded palms in air;
> I only know I cannot drift
> Beyond His love and care.[6]

Another poet who, like Whittier, longed to see again old friends who had died was the Scottish writer John Gibson Lockhart, best known for his biography of his father-in-law, Walter Scott. In a poem written around 1842 and included in a letter to Thomas Carlyle, he too used the imagery of the distant shore to convey the idea of the heaven that he desperately wanted to believe in:

But 'tis an old belief
That on some solemn shore
Beyond the sphere of grief
Dear friends shall meet once more:

Beyond the sphere of Time
And Sin and Fate's control,
Serene in endless prime
Of body and of soul.

That creed I fain would keep,
That hope I'll not forgo—
Eternal be the sleep
Unless to waken so![7]

Philosophers might perhaps be expected to be more sceptical than poets. Yet several of the most prominent Victorian freethinkers among them clung on to a hope and vision of heaven, none more so than the man dubbed by Gladstone "the Saint of Rationalism" and often thought of, not least because of some of his own best-known utterances, as an unbeliever and atheist. John Stuart Mill observed in his autobiography that he was a rarity in the nineteenth century because he had not lost his religious beliefs but never had any, being a freethinker from beginning to end. Yet as Timothy Larsen has very clearly demonstrated in his recent biography, Mill, although a religious sceptic, had an abiding knowledge of and attachment to the Bible, a fondness for church buildings and liturgies and a highly sympathetic approach to many of the central tenets of Christianity. In an essay entitled "Theism", written in 1868–70 and published after his death, on the basis of which Larsen dubs him a "probabilist theist", Mill writes that "there is a large balance of probability" in favour of there being a Creator. He also commends much in the life and teaching of Jesus and even seems to accept him as having some kind of Messianic status.

Mill was certainly open to the possibility of immortality. In 1834, he wrote to Thomas Carlyle, "With respect to the immortality of the soul, I see no reason to believe that it perishes, nor sufficient evidence for complete assurance that it survives."[8] Six years later he wrote to his friend Barclay Fox, "What we call our bodily sensations are all in the mind & would not necessarily or probably cease because the body perishes."[9] In "Theism", which could be said to constitute his last will and testament, he sounds a reasonably positive note about the prospect of a life beyond this one, even if it remained for him a distinct possibility rather than a certainty: "There is, therefore, in science, no evidence against the immortality of the soul but that negative evidence, which consists in the absence of evidence in its favour. And even the negative evidence is not so strong as negative evidence often is."[10]

Benjamin Jowett (1817–93), the celebrated Master of Balliol College, Oxford, who possessed one of the best minds of the Victorian age, stands somewhat apart from the other intellectuals considered in this chapter in that he was an Anglican clergyman with a reasonably orthodox if markedly liberal Christian faith. That at least is the conclusion of his modern biographer, Peter Hinchliff, although his contemporary, Henry Scott Holland, summed up Jowett's faith as "just Platonism flavoured with a little Christian charity".[11] A close friend of Tennyson, Jowett was deeply influenced by *In Memoriam* He finds a place here among those of a more agnostic and free-thinking persuasion because of the way he wrestled intellectually with questions of faith and belief, not least in respect of death and what may lie beyond it.

Jowett pondered the subject of the afterlife most deeply in the introduction to his translation of Plato's *Phaedro*, begun in 1871 but not published until 1892. Observing that "the doctrine of the immortality of the soul has sunk deep into the heart of the human race", he notes that for most of history it had essentially been "a customary rather than a reasoned belief". In recent times, however, "the whole question has been reopened". Scientific advances, including the theory of evolution, the rise of biblical criticism and the waning authority of the Church have combined to weaken the hold of the traditional picture of heaven as a place where white-robed angelic choirs surrounded the throne of God. In the new scientific age, "in which the rules of evidence are stricter and the mind has become more sensitive to criticism", it is no longer tenable to advance "arguments derived from material things such as the seed and the ear of corn or transitions in the life of animals from one state of being to another (the chrysalis and the butterfly)". The evidence for the historical fact of Christ's resurrection "also seems to be weaker than was once supposed: it is not consistent with itself, and is based upon documents which are of unknown origin".[12]

Yet despite what he regards as the dissolution of these traditional props and arguments for immortality, so many of which were still being employed by his contemporaries, Jowett does not want to ditch belief in a future life:

> Though we cannot altogether shut out the childish fear that the soul upon leaving the body may 'vanish into thin air', we have still a hope of immortality with which we comfort ourselves on sufficient grounds. The denial of this belief takes the heart out of human life. As Goethe says, 'He is dead even in this world who has no belief in another.'[13]

How could the idea of heaven be best conveyed in a contemporary and meaningful way? Insisting that the doctrine of immortality must be grounded on the nature of God and the "first principles of morality", Jowett argues for a move away from envisaging heaven in terms of traditional pictures and images to a much more intellectual approach based on ideas and concepts:

> It is clear that to our minds the risen soul can no longer be described, as in a picture, by the symbol of a creature half bird, half human, nor in any other form of sense. The multitude of angels, as in Milton, singing the Almighty's praises, are a noble image, and may furnish a theme for the poet or the painter, but they are no longer an adequate expression of the kingdom of God which is within us. Neither is there any mansion, in this world or another, in which the departed can be imagined to dwell and carry on their occupations. When this earthly tabernacle is dissolved, no other habitation or building can take them in.
>
> It is in the language of ideas only that we can speak of the departed. First of all there is the thought of rest and freedom from pain; they have gone home, as the common saying is, and the cares

of this world touch them no more. Secondly, we may imagine them as they were at their best and brightest, humbly fulfilling their daily round of duties—selfless, childlike, unaffected by the world; when the eye was single and the whole body seemed to be full of light; when the mind was clear and saw into the purposes of God. Thirdly, we may think of them as possessed by a great love of God and man, working out His will at a further stage in the heavenly pilgrimage. And yet we acknowledge that these are the things which eye hath not seen nor ear heard. Fourthly, there may have been some moments in our own lives when we have risen above ourselves, or been conscious of our truer selves, in which the will of God has superseded our wills, and we have entered into communion with Him, and been partakers for a brief season of the Divine truth and love, in which like Christ we have been inspired to utter the prayer, 'I in them, and thou in me, that we may be all made perfect in one.' These precious moments, if we have ever known them, are the nearest approach we can make to the idea of immortality.[14]

Despite Jowett's determination to adopt a rigorously intellectual and modern approach, the above set of ideas about heaven is a curious amalgam of traditional and more novel philosophical approaches. His first one, focusing on rest and freedom from pain and the image of heaven as home, is totally consonant with the language of the comforting Sunday school hymns of which in other respects he seems so dismissive. His second idea, in which souls in heaven are imagined "as they were at their best and brightest, humbly fulfilling their daily round of duties", conforms with the widespread Victorian perception of heaven as an extension of earth where the daily round and common task of earthly life is continued. His fourth conception of immortality as a state of closeness and submission to God's will which can be achieved as much in this world as in the next strongly echoes F. D. Maurice and anticipates the realized eschatology of much twentieth-century theology with its emphasis on achieving immortality here and now.

What is perhaps most striking about Jowett's conception of heaven in the extract above is the third thought that he expresses about it, in which the souls of the departed are conceived as working out God's will "at a further stage in the heavenly pilgrimage". Even more than Maurice, Jowett views heaven as a place, or perhaps rather more a state, of continuous progress and development, a celestial seminary-cum-university in which all souls would be on a track to moral and intellectual improvement:

> The truest conception which we can form of a future life is a state of progress or education—a progress from evil to good, from ignorance to knowledge. To this we are led by the analogy of the present life, in which we see different races and nations of men, and different men and women of the same nation, in various states or stages of cultivation; some more and some less developed, and all of them capable of improvement under favourable circumstances.[15]

Ultimately Jowett grounds his belief in heaven and his view of what it would be like on his understanding of the nature and purpose of God. God embodies perfection, and it is His will that humans should themselves attain perfection. That process begins in this world, but it is very incomplete here, and it is inconceivable that it ends with death: "God cannot have given us capacities and affections that they should find no other fulfilment than they attain here."[16] Jowett is emphatic that we become united to God "not by mystical absorption, but by partaking, whether consciously or unconsciously, of that truth and justice and love which He himself is". Jowett views heaven as existing primarily for the purpose of strenuous moral and intellectual progress:

> The belief in the immortality of the soul rests at last on the belief in God. If there is a good and wise God, then there is a progress of mankind towards perfection; and if there is no progress of men towards perfection, then there is no good and wise God. We cannot suppose that the moral government of God of which we see the beginnings in the world and in ourselves will cease when we pass out of life.[17]

Somewhat similar views about heaven to Jowett's were held by Francis Newman (1805–97), another formidable Victorian intellectual who moved in a very different direction theologically from his better-known elder brother, John Henry. While he clung on longer to the Evangelicalism in which they had both been reared, was briefly a Baptist and went as a missionary to Baghdad, Francis later espoused Unitarianism and ended up as a prominent secularist and freethinker. In an early book, *The Soul, its Sorrows and Aspirations*, published in 1849, described by his brother John Henry as "a dreadful work ... denying Scripture as a whole to be true", he tears into the doctrine of eternal punishment and argues that any doctrine of eternal life could not be based on the supposed resurrection of Christ. Ten years later, he wrote more fully about the future life in a prose poem, *Theism, Doctrinal and Practical*, suggesting that belief in it should be grounded in a kind of moral idealism rather than on traditional Christian doctrine.

In fact, Francis Newman had a profound respect for what he called the Christian vision of heaven and praised its selflessness, writing in an essay of 1872:

> The peculiarity of the Christian vision [of heaven] is that it has no form or comeliness to the worldly mind, the fierce or hard heart, the meanly ambitious, nor to any who are absorbed in self and contented in sin.
> 
> Many a scoffer has said of it, 'It is tiresome enough to sing long hymns at church; I should not like at all to be harping and trumpeting day and night on a cloud.' The scoffer does not go on to confess, yet it is nonetheless true, that he has no pleasure in anticipating a land of universal holiness, where every eye looks up with love and joy to the guiding countenance of a righteous Lord. It needs a heart essentially in love with holiness, whatever its sins from bursts of uncontrolled passion, to make the Christian heaven seem desirable.
> 
> There is here no vulgar notion of thrones and crowns and sitting on an upper seat, which, scattered here and there in the New Testament, damages the doctrine, and does but gratify ambition; there is no exaltation of self; but, as a mother desires to

> see the happiness and honour of her son, most unselfishly, so does the spiritual Christian aspire to see the reign of righteousness and holiness triumphant. Faith in such a Paradise, *just as in proportion as it can be sustained*, seems to me undeniably sanctifying and ennobling.[18]

Here Francis finds himself in total agreement with his brother John Henry's conviction that "holiness is necessary for future blessedness".[19] He also echoes George Matheson's belief that it is loss of ego and of self-love which will define the heavenly condition. What makes him uneasy the depictions of heaven in the New Testament, especially in the Book of Revelation, and seized on by his contemporaries, which he felt were too spiritual, ethereal, hierarchical and static. Conceding that "as beautiful visions, they have an ennobling tendency", he worries that they are altogether too sentimental and that "if they be confidently accepted as true, while they are not true", they could be very dangerous and encourage a passive, submissive, pie-in-the-sky mentality.[20] Comparing different cultural constructions of the afterlife, he writes, "While the heaven of Cicero was all intellect, the heaven of the American Indian all action, the heaven of historical Christianity is all devout sentiment. No one of these can be the true heaven."[21]

Francis Newman acknowledges that it is much easier for the uneducated "rude" mind to believe in this kind of heaven than it is for an intellectual like him beset with questions and doubts. Like Jowett, he wants a much more bracing and challenging afterlife which would involve moral and intellectual advancement. In his 1886 book *Life after Death*, he wrote:

> I have never particularly wished to go to the Christian Heaven. It is certainly too monotonous for an Eternity. The negative side of it sounds all right. Absence of pain, of mental disquiet, of cold and heat, of hunger and thirst, of turmoil and contention, of toil and weariness, of sin and death,—thus much I understand, and for a moment approve; but all this is completely provided in the old Hebrew grave, without any after-life. To make a new life desirable, it must give us something to do, something worth

striving for, and a career by which we may improve in Virtue. If we are to retain active powers, we need some objects that worthily call out those powers. If we are to increase in virtue, we need occasions for self-denial, self-control, and self-sacrifice. Want and pain, toil and trial, cannot be wholly banished out of my Heaven.[22]

Newman is with Jowett in wanting heaven to be a place of continuous and progressive self-development. "Man's virtue, as known to us," he writes, "is progressive; and to imagine that by death the human being can leap into absolute divine perfection is very implausible. Higher and higher progress is all that can reasonably be hoped for."[23] Where he goes beyond Jowett is in his insistence that there must be real pain and suffering in heaven if it really is to be a place of moral growth and advancement:

> The idea that pain is totally excluded from heaven assumes that pain in itself, and in whatever degree, is an essential evil. When pain conduces to moral advancement, it must be accounted a good; and it does most visibly exercise and cement affection, and excite gratitude and love so eminently as to suggest that, if the higher moral attachments of one finite being to another are to exist in heaven, occasional pain and want and feebleness cannot be excluded.[24]

Newman's sense that there is a place for pain in heaven was shared by several other eminent Victorians of a more orthodox Christian faith. George Grove, the polymath best known today as the originator of the musical dictionary which still bears his name, and who was also a talented civil engineer and amateur biblical scholar, argued, "Surely Heaven will be nothing without regret and longing: perfect satisfaction can never be our lot here or there."[25] William Ewart Gladstone, who also believed in what he called the "progressive state" of the "Christian dead", felt heaven would include "an admixture of salutary and accepted pain".[26]

For another prominent freethinker, the journalist and political commentator William Rathbone Greg (1809–81), the Christian doctrine of the resurrection of the body was a barrier rather than an aid to belief in heaven and a future life. Educated in a Unitarian school, Greg was a prominent member of the Plinian Society, which challenged orthodox religious beliefs. In his 1851 book *The Creed of Christendom*, he suggests that there is no real evidence for Christ's resurrection. Even had it happened, he sees it as offering no real hope for humans:

> For our bodies, like those of the countless generations who have lived and passed away since Christ trod our earth, will have crumbled into dust, and passed into other combinations, and become in turn the bodies of myriads of other animated beings, before the great expected day of resurrection of the just. To us a bodily resurrection is impossible. If, therefore, Christ's resurrection were *spiritual*—independent of his buried body—it might be a type and foreshadowing of our own but if it was corporeal, as the evangelists relate, it is rather an extinguisher than a confirmation of our hopes.[27]

For Greg any hope for immortality rests on ditching the Bible with its improbable and unsatisfactory story of Christ's bodily resurrection: "Our interest, as waiters and hopers for an immortality, would appear to lie in disbelieving the letter of the Scripture narratives."[28] He dismisses the idea of Christianity as a revealed faith, writing that "a future life becomes to us no longer a matter of positive knowledge—a revealed fact—but simply a matter of faith, of hope, of earnest desire, a sublime possibility, round which meditation and inquiry will collect all the probabilities they can".[29] Although profoundly sceptical about the Christian idea of heaven, which he feels is "a belief that has grown out of a wish", he is unwilling to ditch the hope of another life beyond this one: "The intellect can never discover it but the soul must and does perpetually reveal it."[30] For him, if there is indeed an existence beyond death it must be an essentially spiritual one. This life is all about action and duty—"Man's spirituality will come in the next stage of his being ... the body will be dropped to death but the soul will go on."[31]

Like Francis Newman, William Greg is insistent that heaven, if it does indeed exist, must be a progressive state: "It is unreasonable to expect so entire a change in the character of the soul, by the mere event of death, as would entitle it, or enable it, to enter at once on the enjoyment of supreme felicity." Rather, the soul "through long ages of self-elaborating effort, must win its way up nearer and nearer the Throne of God".[32] Life in heaven will be an invigorating, exciting, continuing challenge.

One of the most eminent academic philosophers in late Victorian Britain clung almost desperately to a belief in immortality despite, like Greg, rejecting the tenets of Christianity. Henry Sidgwick (1838–1900), a utilitarian who held the chair of moral philosophy at the University of Cambridge from 1883 until his death, left the Church of England because he could not subscribe to its teaching, but remained a theist and a classic example of the Victorian "honest doubter" who wrestled with questions of faith. In a letter written in 1860 to Alfred Tennyson's son, Hallam, he notes that "the great issues between Agnostic Science and Faith have become continually more prominent" and praises *In Memoriam* for promoting honest doubt and encouraging free and progressive thought:

> Freedom is won, and what does Freedom bring us to? It brings us face to face with atheistic science: the faith in God and Immortality, which we had been struggling to clear from superstition, suddenly seems to be *in the air*: and in seeking for a firm basis for this faith we find ourselves in the midst of the 'fight with death' which 'In Memoriam' so powerfully presents.[33]

Like so many of his contemporaries, Sidgwick could not bring himself to give up believing in and hoping for an afterlife in heaven, even though his rational mind argued against it. Long after he renounced Christianity and left the Church of England he continued to cling to the "sure and certain hope of the resurrection from the dead" promised in the Book of Common Prayer burial service. He spent the last 30 years of his life searching for empirical proof that an afterlife existed and, in company with other Victorians who lost their faith, he resorted to spiritualism, being one of the principal founders of the Society for Psychical Research in 1882. He expressed his own agnosticism on the whole issue, and his reason for not making more of his doubts, in a candid letter written in 1881 to a fellow academic and rationalist, John Rickards Mozley:

The reason why I keep strict silence now for many years with regard to theology is that while I cannot myself discover adequate rational basis for the Christian hope of happy immortality, it seems to me that the general loss of such a hope, from the minds of average human beings as now constituted, would be an evil of which I cannot pretend to measure the extent. I am not prepared to say that the dissolution of the existing social order would follow, but I think the danger of such dissolution would be seriously increased, and that the evil would certainly be very great.[34]

There were many other sensitive Victorian thinkers who similarly hid their doubts about the "hope of happy immortality" out of a concern about the effects on morality and social order if popular belief in the idea of heaven collapsed. But, as with Sidgwick, this was not the only nor perhaps even the overriding reason why they did not come out as outright scoffers and debunkers of the notion of immortality. As this chapter has shown, even the more determined freethinkers, rationalists and secularists could never quite abandon the notion of an immortal soul nor give up faintly trusting the larger hope that "those we call the dead" are, indeed, happy and "breathers of an ampler day for ever nobler ends".

## Notes

[1] *The Works of John Ruskin*, Vol. XXVI (London: George Allen, 1909), pp. 137–8.
[2] Richard Curle, *Robert Browning and Julia Wedgwood: A broken friendship as revealed in their letters* (New York: Frederick Stokes, 1937), p. 7.
[3] Arthur Hugh Clough, *Selected Poems* (Harmondsworth: Penguin Books, 1991), pp. 93–4.
[4] *Poems of Arthur Hugh Clough* (London: Macmillan, 1913), pp. 92–3. These three verses are sadly missing from the Penguin Classics edition of Clough's poems.
[5] Clough, *Selected Poems*, p. 213.

6   *The Poetical Works of John Greenleaf Whittier*, Vol. II (Boston: Houghton Mifflin & Co., 1892), p. 267.
7   Andrew Lang, *The Life and Letters of John Gibson Lockhart*, Vol. 2 (London: John Nimmo, 1897), p. 235.
8   Timothy Larsen, *John Stuart Mill: A Secular Life* (Oxford: Oxford University Press, 2018), p. 260.
9   Larsen, *John Stuart Mill*, p. 260.
10  Larsen, *John Stuart Mill*, p. 205.
11  Peter Hinchliff, *Benjamin Jowett and the Christian Religion* (Oxford: Oxford University Press, 1987), p. 116.
12  Benjamin Jowett (ed.), *The Dialogues of Plato*, Vol. II, 3rd edn (London: Oxford University Press, 1892), pp. 170–1.
13  Jowett (ed.), *The Dialogues of Plato*, Vol. II, p. 180.
14  Jowett (ed.), *The Dialogues of Plato*, Vol. II, p. 182.
15  Jowett (ed.), *The Dialogues of Plato*, Vol. II, p. 183.
16  Benjamin Jowett, *The Interpretation of Scripture, and Other Essays* (London: George Routledge, 1907), p. 98.
17  Jowett (ed.), *The Dialogues of Plato*, Vol. II, p. 182.
18  Francis W. Newman, *On the Vision of Heaven* (Toledo: Index Tracts, 1872), pp. 5–6.
19  Newman, *On the Vision of Heaven*, p. 6.
20  Newman, *On the Vision of Heaven*, p. 7.
21  Newman, *On the Vision of Heaven*, p. 8.
22  F. W. Newman, *Life after Death?* (London: Trübner & Co., 1886), p. 34.
23  Newman, *On the Vision of Heaven*, p. 8.
24  Newman, *On the Vision of Heaven*, p. 8.
25  Charles L. Graves, *The Life and Letters of George Grove* (London: Macmillan, 1903), p. 198.
26  Michael Wheeler, *Death and the Future Life in Victorian Literature and Theology* (Cambridge: Cambridge University Press, 1990), p. 78.
27  William Rathbone Greg, *The Creed of Christendom* (London: John Chapman, 1851), pp. 222–3.
28  Greg, *The Creed of Christendom*, p. 223.
29  Greg, *The Creed of Christendom*, p. 279.
30  Greg, *The Creed of Christendom*, p. 301.
31  Greg, *The Creed of Christendom*, p. 275.

32 Greg, *The Creed of Christendom*, p. 306.
33 Hallam Tennyson, *Alfred Lord Tennyson: A Memoir* (London: Macmillan, 1897), p. 302.
34 Arthur Sidgwick and Eleanor M. Sidgwick, *Henry Sidgwick: A Memoir* (New York: Macmillan, 1906), p. 357. In a rare lapse, Geoffrey Rowell states the recipient of this letter was J. B. Mozley, the High Church theologian who died in 1871, ten years before it was sent.

# Conclusion

As in so many other areas, the twentieth century saw a complete reaction against and reversal of Victorian attitudes towards death and the afterlife. Instead of being the focus of an almost obsessive level of interest and attention, death became taboo, a largely forbidden and neglected topic. There was a concomitant loss of interest in heaven both on the part of academic theologians and in popular consciousness. This dramatic change of outlook from the Victorian mindset lasted for more than 100 years and is only now being challenged.

There are several reasons for this abandonment of Victorian views on death and the afterlife in the twentieth century. The most obvious is the dramatic rise in average life expectancy and fall in infant mortality as a result of medical advances. Death became much less common and many people did not have direct experience of it until reaching late middle age. It also became much less public, with fewer and fewer deaths taking place at home and more and more in curtained-off beds and side wards in hospitals and care homes where many died alone, their bodies taken away by undertakers for cremation.

This privatization of death has been accompanied by its medicalization. Doctors rather than religious practitioners have become its key mediators and interpreters. In Philippe Ariès' words, death has moved from being an occasion loaded with spiritual significance and ritual ceremony to "a technical phenomenon obtained by a cessation of care, a cessation determined in a more or less avowed way by a decision of the doctor and the hospital team".[1] The Israeli philosopher and historian, Yuval Noah Harari, puts it even more graphically, pointing to the change whereby instead of being seen as the main source of meaning of life, death has come to be seen as something that humans can outsmart and defeat:

> We don't need to wait for Christ's second coming in order to overcome death. A couple of scientists in a lab can do it. Whereas traditionally death was the speciality of priests and theologians in black cassocks, now it's the folks in white lab coats ... The best human minds no longer spend their time trying to give meaning to death. Instead, they are busy extending life.[2]

As Harari says, the medicalization of death has led to a general presumption in favour of preserving and prolonging life at all costs. In many ways this has been positive, giving many people extra years of life and eliminating killer diseases. But it has also had a more negative effect, putting the emphasis on the quantity rather than quality of life, prolonging the experience of dying, which has become a much more drawn out affair than it was in the nineteenth century, and encouraging the view, both in the medical profession and more generally, that death is something to be avoided and that it represents a failure when it occurs.

The beginnings of this change of attitude can be seen in one of the first "great deaths" of the twentieth century, that of the 8th Duke of Argyll, who died on 24 April 1900 in his ancestral home of Inveraray Castle in Scotland after a painful, protracted terminal illness during which doctors worked hard to keep him alive by administering oxygen and injecting strychnine. As Pat Jalland has commented, this was very much a twentieth-century rather than a nineteenth-century death, being perhaps the first documented one in which members of the medical profession repudiated what had been the standard Victorian practice of favouring euthanasia and not seeking to prolong life with drugs and other interventions.[3] It established a precedent which was increasingly followed through the twentieth century.

In marked contrast to the Victorian view, death became something to be feared and avoided rather than something to be celebrated. Indeed, it came to replace sex as the great taboo and unmentionable and forbidden topic. Partly in reaction to what was admittedly excessive grieving and mourning on the part of the Victorians, the twentieth century saw sorrow and grief being choked back and bottled up and mourning rituals discarded or pared back to a bare minimum. Fear and terror of death replaced familiarity and acceptance, not just in Britain but across the so-called developed world, as commented on by Sogyal Rinpoche, the Buddhist author of *The Tibetan Book of Living and Dying* (1992), when he wrote, "Wherever I go in the West, I am struck by the great mental suffering that arises from the fear of dying... modern western society has no real understanding of death or what happens in death or after death."[4]

In tandem with this shutting up and shutting out of death went a greatly diminished concern about what might follow it, something that was further encouraged by the accelerating loss of religious faith throughout the twentieth century. Questions around the existence of an afterlife and the nature of heaven that had excited almost universal interest at its start became by its end a matter of general indifference. It is not difficult to find testaments and witnesses to this gradual loss of belief in life beyond death. In his celebrated Gifford Lectures in Edinburgh in 1901–2 that became the basis for his seminal book *The Varieties of Religious Experience*, William James, the American philosopher and psychologist, could confidently state that "religion for the great majority of our own race means immortality and nothing else".[5] James Frazer, the pioneer Scottish anthropologist, wrote in even more ringing terms in his 1913 book *The Belief in Immortality* that the idea of life after death "must rank among the most firmly established of truths—were it put to the vote, it would command an overwhelming majority across humanity. The few dissenters would be overborne; their voices would be drowned in the general roar... on this point, sceptical or agnostic peoples are nearly, if not wholly unknown."[6] Over successive decades, the number of people continuing to adhere to this "most firmly established of truths" steadily declined. George Orwell noted in 1944 that belief in survival after death "is enormously less widespread than it was".[7]

The declining interest and belief in existence beyond death is clearly indicated in the writings of major twentieth-century theologians. It has been well documented by Donald MacEwan, chaplain to the University of St Andrews, in his 2000 doctoral thesis *Missing Persons: Individual Eschatology in Twentieth Century Protestant Eschatology*. He demonstrates how the four leading Protestant theologians of the twentieth century, Rudolf Bultmann, Karl Barth, Jürgen Moltmann and Eberhard Jüngel, have no interest in heaven and reject the idea that humans have an immortal soul. Barth is quoted as saying that "in death man is only the spent soul of a spent body ... We shall die. This, and nothing else, will be the end awaiting us", and Moltmann that "the soul does not soar above our vale of tears to some magical heavenly bliss".[8]

For MacEwan, "twentieth-century theology turns its back on immortality ... There is no attempt to develop an account of loving, knowing subjects beyond death, hence the missing persons of this title."[9] What he describes is a radical departure on the part of mainstream Protestant theology from the ideas of nineteenth-century Anglicans, Scottish Presbyterians and Nonconformists as expressed and explored in this book. In his words:

> God may dwell in eternity; God may not cease to exist with every human death; but what of the individual? Will he or she continue to live beyond death? Will such life involve knowledge and love of God and others? The twentieth-century Protestants answer these questions at best, ambivalently, at worst, with a short shake of the head.[10]

In so far as it has dealt with eschatology, much late-twentieth-century Protestant theology has sought to eliminate what is seen as the alien Platonic idea of the immortality of the soul from Christian thinking altogether and instead focus solely on the resurrection of the body. This is evident in the writings of Oscar Cullmann, Eberhard Jüngel, and in England in particular in the work of N. T. Wright with his insistence that our hope after death consists "not in going on for ever and ever, not in an endless cycle of death and rebirth as in Stoicism, not in a blessed disembodied mortal existence, but in a newly embodied life, a transformed physicality".[11]

There has been some serious and sympathetic engagement with the notion of immortality by a handful of late-twentieth-century British theologians who have not been prepared to ditch it completely. Paul Badham, a liberal Anglican priest who spent most of his career at the University of Lampeter, has devoted several books to the subject and come down (just) in favour of immortality and eternal life and a belief that "it is still possible to spell out the Christian hope in ways that are reasonable".[12] He has the strong pastoral instincts of the Victorian Broad

Churchmen (shown in his support for assisted dying) and shares their tentativeness and hesitancy, writing that hope in a future life "can no longer be securely based on the integrated framework of traditional Christian doctrine".[13] He takes seriously the phenomena of near death experiences, claimed memories of former lives and evidence from psychical research. Ultimately, he grounds his hope for future life on religious experience, arguing that "the experience of God requires life beyond death", and is sympathetic to the idea that our post-death or eternal future lies in being remembered by, or being held in, God's memory.[14]

John Hick, the distinguished philosopher of religion who started out as a Presbyterian minister and ended his life as a Quaker, follows nineteenth-century thinkers (although he does not reference them) in seeing the self and individuality surviving after death but transcending the ego so that eternal life becomes entry into a common vision of God and an eternal consciousness of divine reality. He is happy with the idea of an intermediate state during which souls will be perfected. He also has a nineteenth-century outlook in finding the idea of hell "morally intolerable". Appropriately for one who devoted so much of his time to seeking to understand and engage with eastern religions, he argues for an alternative possibility to either eternal heaven or hell, or repeated earthly incarnations, "namely a series of lives, each bounded by something analogous to birth and death, lived in other worlds in spaces other than that in which we now are":

> This hypothesis accepts both the insistence upon the need for life to be lived within temporal limits and the conviction that the soul can only make progress in the incarnate state towards its final goal. But it differs from the western tradition in postulating many lives instead of only one, and from the eastern tradition in postulating many spheres of Incarnate existence instead of only one.
>
> It may then be that in progressively 'higher' worlds (i.e. worlds which are the environments of evermore morally and spiritually perfect modes of existence) the interpersonality of mutual love becomes the universal principle of life, whilst self protective egoity withers away, so that the individual's series of

lives culminates eventually in a last life beyond which there is no further embodiment but instead entry into the common Vision of God, or Nirvana, or the eternal consciousness of the atman in its relation to Ultimate Reality.[15]

Several prominent twentieth-century Roman Catholic theologians have written positively about immortality and eternal life. Karl Rahner, who maintained an interest in the subject throughout his career, argued in his 1961 treatise *On The Theology of Death* that "the personal, spiritual soul does not perish when the structure of the body is dissolved, but maintains its personal life".[16] While insisting on the continued individual and personal identity of each soul after death, he further argues that, released from the limitation of its exclusive relationship to a human body, the soul will instead become related to the entire universe: "In death, the soul becomes not acosmic but pancosmic."[17] Traditional ideas of immortality and eternal life have also received sympathetic if critical treatment in Hans Urs von Balthasar's *The Last Act* (1983) and Simon Tugwell's *Human Immortality and the Redemption of Death* (1990).

Perhaps the most interesting modern work by a Roman Catholic theologian is Hans Küng's *Eternal Life?*, published in German in 1982 and in an English translation in 1984. Küng is one of the few modern theologians actually to engage with the idea of heaven, to which he devotes a chapter in his book. He begins by reflecting that "what formerly represented the great questions of our whence and whither, our all-embracing happiness" has suffered from and been devalued by "the presumption of astronomers" and the casual ways in which the word is invoked in moments of embarrassment and anger and "made to serve as a theme for uninspired popular songs and cheap moonlight romanticism". Yet despite all this, the word heaven "has retained its archetypal religious meaning and is in any case not so easy to replace by something different or better". Seeking to find "an ultimate reality in which we of the twentieth century can believe and in which we can trust", he goes on to state his view that the heaven of faith is not a "supramundane 'above' . . . nor an extramundane 'beyond' . . . not a place, but a mode of being . . . the heaven of faith is nothing other than the hidden, invisible, incomprehensible sphere of God which, far from being out of reach of earth, completes everything in good".

Küng almost seems to hark back to the poetic, imaginative voices of the Victorians in what he says next:

> What can belief in a heaven mean for us? Heaven always has something to do with our fantasies and dreams, with what is marginal in our life, with what remains unsettled. Articulation of resurrection hope implies also the courage to stand by our dreams, however private or intimate these may be. How much is involved here of what is personal, unadmitted, inexpressible![18]

After this romantic reflection, Küng ends his chapter on heaven with a poem by the German writer Marie Luise Kaschnitz which begins (in its English translation): "Do you believe, they asked me,/In a life after death?/And I answered: Yes./But I could not explain/What it might look like." Küng ends his book with a ringing endorsement of eternal life, seemingly at odds with the Tennysonian question mark in the title, a strong affirmation of universalism and a looking forward to God being all in all in some wonderful consummation which will bring true happiness to all humanity. He is content to find this spelled out in the new heaven and new earth promised in the Book of Revelation which he takes very literally. In many ways, he comes closer than any other modern theologian to the Victorian thinkers who have been the subject of this book, not least in his use of poetic imagination and his hope-filled idealism.

Although Rahner, Küng, Badham, Hick and others have kept alive the flame of immortality and eternal life, it remains true that heaven has largely disappeared from recent Christian theology. In their book *Heaven: A History*, Bernhard Lang and Colleen McDannell write that "scientific, philosophical and theological scepticism has nullified the modern heaven and replaced it with teachings that are minimalist, meagre and dry".[19] Lang has subsequently expanded this analysis, noting that:

> twentieth-century theology has not been kind to the notion of heaven as the abode of the blessed. While in certain circles nineteenth-century notions of heavenly homes persist, most

theologians (such as Rahner and Barth) describe heavenly existence in minimalist fashion... Some radical theologians have gone so far as to denying individual life after death altogether or they are content with vague notions of individual human biographies being forever stored in God's eternal memory.[20]

There are several possible reasons for this widespread abandonment of heaven by twentieth-century theologians. Donald MacEwan sees it as the result of the collapse of natural theology and an exclusive concentration on revealed theology. Brian Hebblethwaite, an Anglican theologian who has done much to try and synthesize the notion of the immortality of the soul and the doctrine of resurrection, prefers a philosophical explanation for the rejection of the traditional Christian hope of immortality. For him, it comes from "the modern sense of human life as an essentially bounded affair—the boundaries of birth and death prescribing the very nature and conditions of human existence in its finitude and temporality. This view found philosophical expression in the work of Heidegger, who insisted on 'being towards death' as a defining characteristic of the human".[21]

Heaven has also undoubtedly been downgraded in Christian thinking thanks to a focus on what is technically called realized eschatology, the idea that the kingdom of heaven is realized here and now and that the emphasis of theology should be on this world rather than the next. Much of this is a very laudable reaction against what is taken to be the escapist, over-spiritualized and ethereal pie-in-the-sky theology of the Victorians, which accepted inequality, poverty and oppression on the grounds that it would be sorted out in heaven. Much twentieth-century theology focuses rather on the social gospel, and on areas such as liberation, feminism and the environment, exhorting Christians to fight for justice, peace, equality and the integrity of creation, as epitomized by the Christian Aid slogan "We believe in life before death". This wholly understandable and in many ways very positive move has meant much less focus on death and what may follow it.

This avoidance and downplaying of heaven did not come to an end with the renewed pastoral interest in death and dying which occurred in the latter decades of the twentieth century. What has been dubbed "the modern death awareness movement" is often taken as beginning with the publication of the very influential study *On Death and Dying* by the Swiss-American psychiatrist Elisabeth Kübler-Ross in 1969. Its emphasis is on the processes of dying and grieving rather than on death itself and it had almost no interest in the afterlife. For Kübler-Ross, what follows death is mourning rather than life eternal. Her ideas, and the writings of her disciples, became the basis for most Christian teaching and thinking about death and especially for the pastoral training of the clergy in the late twentieth and early twenty-first century. As Lucy Bregman, Emeritus Professor at Temple University, Philadelphia, who has written much about the theology of death and dying, puts it:

> Today, if one wants to learn what Christians are saying about death and dying, the bulk of pastoral-care writings are shaped much less by traditional theological concerns than by the work of Kübler-Ross and her followers. Dealing with one's own impending death is modelled on 'loss', with major attention given to mourners. A book by a Christian pastoral care expert entitled *Surviving Death* focuses on these two situations exclusively: no mention of any afterlife, positive or negative, can be found in its pages. Funeral sermons have now become 'preaching to mourners', another title that indicates this shift away from traditional topics. Moreover, the medicalization of death means that much Christian reflection on dying focuses on bioethics, hospice and end of life care: all very important, but not directly connected to traditional theological themes surrounding death.[22]

The opening decades of the twenty-first century have seen signs of the beginning of a significant change in attitude to death, not least on the part of the medical profession. Following the lead given in the 2014 BBC Reith Lectures by Dr Atwul Gawande, an American surgeon, doctors are increasingly questioning the wisdom of trying to prolong human life at all costs. Baroness Black of Strome, better known as Dame Sue Black, the eminent forensic pathologist, has bemoaned the fact that we have "fallen out of love with death", something she attributes to the fact that most people do not directly encounter it until late middle age. She commends the approach of the Victorians and wants us to return to their celebration and valuing of death as we do birth.[23] There is a lively national debate, in which doctors are taking a prominent role on both sides, about assisted dying. Another sign of a greater openness to death has been the spectacular success of the death café movement. In 2011 Jon Underwood set up the first death café at his home in Hackney as a place where people "could drink tea, eat cake and discuss death". There are now over 12,000 death cafés in 75 countries.

If death is now at last coming out of the closet and being more openly discussed and even embraced, it is also becoming more common and ubiquitous. The Covid-19 pandemic dramatically pushed up death rates across Britain as throughout the world—the annual excess mortality recorded in countries across the European Union in 2022 was more than 10 per cent higher than the 2016–19 average. The pandemic also greatly raised the profile of death with stark statistics of mortality appearing daily in newspapers and news bulletins. Quite apart from the consequences of Covid and its aftermath, there are other long-term demographic trends, notably the impact of an ageing population, which will significantly increase the number of deaths in the coming decades. It has been calculated that the number of deaths in England and Wales will increase by 25 per cent between 2016 and 2040. If current trends continue, there will also be a significant increase in the number of deaths occurring at home and in care homes (up from 35 per cent in 2004 to 69 per cent in 2040) and a corresponding decrease in deaths in hospital (from 51 per cent in 2011 to 22 per cent in 2040).[24]

So there is going to be more death around, and it is going to be a more present reality and less hidden away. In these respects, we are becoming more like the Victorians. However, it is not expected that there will be a rise in infant mortality and very few families are likely to suffer the loss of young children. Indeed, our parents will continue to live on until we ourselves are well beyond the life expectancy of the Victorian age and many people will still not directly encounter death until they reach their sixties. For these reasons, it is unlikely that death will loom anything like as large in our consciousness over coming decades as it did for those who lived 150 and more years ago. Yuval Noah Harari, the Israeli philosopher and historian quoted at the beginning of this chapter, has speculated whether Covid will change our modern belief that humans can defeat death and return us to more traditional, accepting attitudes. He concludes that if anything, it is more likely to reinforce the view of death as a medical challenge to be cheated and fought rather than a spiritual and philosophical reality to be accepted:

> Will the pandemic change human attitudes to death? Probably not. Just the opposite. Covid-19 will probably cause us only to double our efforts to protect human lives . . . For centuries people used religion as a defence mechanism, believing that they would exist for ever in the afterlife. Now people switch to using science as an alternative defence mechanism, believing that doctors will always save them, and that they will live for ever in their apartment . . . When the Covid crisis is over, I don't expect we will see a significant increase in the budgets of philosophy or theology departments. But I bet we will see a massive increase in the budgets of medical schools and healthcare systems.[25]

There are, however, signs of a radical questioning of the medicalization of death, not least from within the medical profession itself. It is the central theme of an important and detailed report produced in 2022 by a commission set up by the medical journal *The Lancet* and entitled "The Value of Death". Members of the commission came not just from the medical profession, especially those involved in hospice and palliative care, but also included faith leaders and academics in other disciplines such as philosophy and sociology. The report's starting point and guiding proposition is that "our relationship with death and dying has become unbalanced and needs to be rebalanced". It begins by outlining the radical changes that have taken place over recent generations in how most people die:

> Death comes later in life for many and dying is often prolonged. Death and dying have moved from a family and community setting to primarily the domain of health systems. Futile or potentially inappropriate treatment can continue into the last hours of life . . . There is an excessive focus on clinical

> interventions at the end of life ... Health care and individuals appear to struggle to accept the inevitability of death.

It goes on:

> Philosophers and theologians from around the globe have recognized the value that death holds for human life. Death and life are bound together: without death there would be no life. Death allows new ideas and new ways. Death also reminds us of our fragility and sameness: we all die. Caring for the dying is a gift not a duty. Much of the value of death is no longer recognized in the modern world. Rediscovering this value can help care at the end of life and enhance living.[26]

Although the Lancet Commission report betokens a welcome opening up to the value of death, not least on the part of the medical profession, there is very little in it about the possibility of an afterlife and the implications that hope of this would have both for the dying and for those caring for them and preparing them for it. It does acknowledge that as well as being seen simply as the end of life, the opposite of health, and a failure (as it still is for many doctors and healthcare professionals), death can also be viewed as "an escape from the suffering of life" and a "gateway to Heaven".[27] There is a brief summary of the attitudes of the main world faiths as to what happens after death which includes this somewhat curt and outdated encapsulation of the Christian view: "Christianity preaches an afterlife in which after the Day of Judgement the good will reside eternally in heaven, while the sinful will be sent to hell."[28] While this is a reasonably accurate statement of traditional orthodox Christian teaching, it will strike many modern Christians as over-emphasizing judgment and hell and hardly reflects nineteenth-century, let alone twentieth-century, thinking on the subject. Hell does not seem to have gone away despite its apparent near-banishment in the Victorian era.

If we are seeing the beginnings of a change in the way that death is perceived, and an end to it being the great forbidden and taboo subject to be hushed up and swept under the carpet, can we expect also to see a greater interest in and openness to the possibility of an afterlife? Is heaven due for a comeback?

An extensive opinion poll undertaken in October 2021 and entitled "the YouGov Death Study: Britons on Life after Death" found that a third of Britons (33 per cent) believe in an afterlife, four in ten (42 per cent) do not, and a quarter (26 per cent) don't know. Women (38 per cent) are more likely than men (26 per cent) to believe in life after death. Belief in life after death falls with increasing age—from 39 per cent among 16–24-year-olds to just 28 per cent of those in their sixties or older, with men experiencing a more marked loss of belief as they age than women.

As might be expected, the YouGov poll reveals a significant difference between religious believers and others. Among those who affirm and actively practise a religious faith, 69 per cent say that they believe in an afterlife and only 11 per cent do not. For those who say they are not religious, the comparable proportions are 17 per cent and 59 per cent.

Among those who say that they do believe in an afterlife, the largest proportion (43 per cent) think that the soul goes to heaven or a similar place where it lives on. One in six (16 per cent) believe in reincarnation and 6 per cent believe in becoming a spirit. A further 22 per cent say they believe there is something after death but are not sure what. Of those who affirm and practise a religious faith, seven in ten (71 per cent) say that the soul continues to live on in heaven or a similar place. Among those who profess no religious faith, 11 per cent believe that the soul lives on in heaven and 30 per cent believe in reincarnation.

The response to a more direct question about belief in the existence of heaven or hell is rather less affirmative. Twelve per cent of all respondents say that they believe only in heaven, with a further 18 per cent saying they believe in both heaven and hell, and over half (54 per cent) saying that they do not believe in either. Among those who affirm and practise a religious faith, one in four (26 per cent) believe only in heaven, nearly half (47 per cent) believe in both heaven and hell, and one in eight (13 per cent) don't believe in either.[29]

These statistics need to be treated with some caution. Opinion polls are not always reliable; they fluctuate quite widely, and they can often be self-contradictory. Both the UK Religion Survey undertaken in 2017 for the BBC and a poll conducted by the Policy Institute at King's College,

London, in 2022 registered a rather higher level of belief in life after death (46 per cent in each case). The 2022 poll found that 41 per cent of Britons believe in heaven and 26 per cent in hell. It confirmed the YouGov Death Survey's findings that belief in an afterlife declines with age (from 51–53 per cent among younger generations to 35–39 per cent among older ones). What is striking about all three recent surveys is the significant number of people who still believe in hell. In the 2022 poll, 32 per cent of respondents under 40 said that they believed in hell, although the proportion dropped to 18 per cent among those aged between 59 and 77. As we have already noted in relation to its prominent mention in the Lancet Commission Report, hell seems not to have disappeared from popular consciousness as much as one might have thought, or hoped.

Other polls suggest that belief in heaven is stronger than belief in God both among the general population and among those who identify as Christians, just over half of whom (56 per cent) say that they believe in the existence of God compared with 71 per cent who say that they believe the soul lives on in heaven.

There is no doubt that people want to talk, read and think about the existence of heaven and what it might be like. It is a favourite topic for discussion in death cafés. In my own experience, it is a subject that particularly engages those thinking about their own mortality or close to death and the grieving relatives of loved ones who have died. They are often initially reticent and hesitant about bringing it up, but it is clear that it weighs heavily on their minds. Over recent years, I have found myself increasingly being asked about death and what may come after it. It was partly to answer such questions that I put together my anthology, *The Quiet Haven: An Anthology of Readings on Death and Heaven* (2021), which includes a considerable number of poems, prayers and meditations by Victorian authors, a good many of whom have been featured and quoted again in more detail in these pages.

The desire of those close to death to talk about heaven is often commented on by hospice chaplains and others involved in end-of-life care. Reflecting on her work as chaplain to communities in Edinburgh living with HIV-Aids, Marion Chatterley, a priest in the Scottish Episcopal Church, writes:

> People want to believe that they will go to heaven, a place that offers unlimited delights for body and mind ... Inevitably, these thoughts lead to discussions about life after death. People often initiate conversations about angels and the connexion between heaven and earth. A number have described profound experiences when they have made a connexion with a loved one who is long deceased ... this can lead to an interest in spiritualism which, in turn, regularly disappoints. Opportunities can be created for conversations about Christian love and hope.[30]

As Marion Chatterley observes, both angels and spiritualism have a strong contemporary appeal. Polls consistently show that around a third of the population believe in angels and around a fifth believe that it is possible to contact the dead through mediums, séances and Ouija boards. Spiritualism is undergoing a boom, although not on the scale that it did in the latter half of the nineteenth century. So is interest in near-death experiences (NDEs), on which there is now an extensive literature. Many of these NDEs seem to involve experiences of something close to classic ideas of heaven, with those who have survived them describing going down a tunnel, being drawn by a great light, floating on clouds and having an overwhelming feeling of being welcomed and coming home. Common to most of those who have had NDEs is a loss of fear of death and a belief that when it does come, they will survive it and go on to another and better life.

To some extent these more esoteric branches of religion have filled the vacuum left by the mainstream churches, which have tended to fight shy of saying much about heaven and left it to mediums, angelologists and interpreters of NDEs to satisfy the growing popular interest in the possibility of an afterlife and what it might be like. There are Christian voices talking about heaven, but they are few and far between and tend to come more from the Catholic rather than the Protestant churches. Peter Stanford, the Catholic writer and journalist, wrote a significant book entitled *Heaven: A Traveller's Guide to an Undiscovered Country* in 2002 in which he called for a re-establishment of the power of myth. He wrote: "Death is not a full stop, exclamation mark, nor, in our own times, a discrete footnote. It is simply the punctuation in the narrative, a question mark that leads on to what we cannot yet read."[31]

The Centre for The Art of Dying Well, an initiative which began with the Catholic Bishops' Conference of England and Wales and is now based at St Mary's University, Twickenham, London, is responsible for a very helpful website created in 2016. As well as providing much sound practical advice, it does not shun the question of life after death. Its section entitled "Questions about Death and Dying" includes this helpful paragraph on "Fear of the Unknown":

> What, if anything, happens after death is a question that may be of particular concern to you right now. Perhaps you believe that there is no life after death—and that is troubling you. Maybe you're really not sure, but you very much hope that there is life beyond the grave for you or your loved one. And even if you have faith in everlasting life, you may find yourself getting 'cold feet' about it.

This section goes on to quote Sister Alice Thomas, a chaplain at King's College Hospital in London:

> Every day, directly or indirectly, patients voice to me their fear of the unknown. I work with many people from many denominations—and also those of no faith—and it's very common for people to be anxious about what happens after death. This is a difficult topic to address generally; it really requires an open conversation with someone about their own private or personal struggles with belief. If the fear of the unknown is troubling someone—whether they have faith or not—I encourage them to open up to a chaplain, priest or minister.

After stating that "the hope Christians have in life after death is rooted in the resurrection of Jesus" and quoting the final prayer of committal at a Catholic funeral in which the priest speaks of "the sure and certain hope of the resurrection to eternal life through our Lord Jesus Christ", the website goes on to take a distinctly Victorian approach to what heaven will be like:

> People with a belief or hope in life after death may also find it comforting to look on death as a reunion. The time has now come to reunite with loved ones who have gone before. If you are dying, you may be saying goodbye to some loved ones, but it means you will also shortly be saying hello to others.[32]

This is one of extremely few twenty-first-century statements that I have come across which talks in clear and confident terms about the reunion of loved ones in heaven and recovers that idea that was so prevalent in Victorian times.

If heaven has received some mention in contemporary Roman Catholic sources and circles, it is conspicuous by its absence in the writings and utterances of liberal Protestants who are the heirs of those Broad Church figures whose thoughts have dominated this book. Some of the greatest exponents of liberal theology in our day are also the most dismissive of any idea of heaven. Typical is the stark comment of Richard Holloway, the former Bishop of Edinburgh and a hero and guru for many of us on the ultra-liberal wing of the Church: "I neither desire nor expect life after death."[33]

This has been commented on by Martin Camroux, a leading liberal theologian in the United Reformed Church and founder of the "Free to Believe" network. In an email in 2018 to members of the network, he wrote:

> Over the years liberals seem to talk less and less about death and what might come after it. In my childhood liberal preachers like Harry Emerson Fosdick and Leslie Weatherhead were happy to preach confident sermons about love's victory over death. Later William Sloane Coffin's Easter sermons were one of the highlights of his ministry at Riverside. Before his own death he said, 'Before every birth and after every death there is still God. The abyss of God's love is deeper than the abyss of death. If we don't know what is beyond the grave, we do know who is beyond the grave.

Today, those on the progressive side of the Church, are by no means as sure whether this is true. Many, including people whose faith I deeply respect, regard any idea of post-death life as an outdated myth. The well-known New Testament theologian Dominic Crossan is one such. He says that, as a Christian, he thinks about life after death, what he thinks about UFOs: he doesn't know and he doesn't care. Crossan's passion is for justice in this world. The afterlife is simply a distraction from what really matters.

Camroux goes on to commend as "a rather refreshing change" from this general attitude the writings of Dale Allison, Professor of New Testament Studies at Princeton Theological Seminary, "a liberal New Testament scholar who emphatically takes a different view". In his 2016 book *Night Comes: Death, Imagination and the Last Things*, Allison notes that we no longer think as much about death as we once did, the idea of bodily resurrection has collapsed and heaven has become less credible. He wants to challenge this prevailing view, as Camroux points out:

> Allison argues that he still expects more after death than a coffin. Christians should imagine the afterlife not as wish fulfilment but as the prospect, perhaps quite painful, of dismantling our egos as we have known them for the sake of something unimaginably larger and more profound than our current individual selves. Christianity without hope beyond death is for him of reduced relevance and of diminished interest. It is not simply a personal matter, something vital is at stake. 'If the brooding grave is everyone's finale, if existence runs into pitiless nothing, then the forgotten and marginalized will remain marginalized and forgotten for all time.' How is that compatible with the God we see in Jesus?[34]

Heaven does still feature in church liturgies, where specific mentions of it are largely to be found in orders for communion services. Prayer D in the Church of England's order for the celebration of Holy Communion in *Common Worship* has the celebrant praying immediately after the epiclesis (invocation of the Holy Spirit) that "all who share this food" may be "welcomed at your feast in heaven", while Prayer E asks God to "bring us with all the saints to feast at your table in heaven".[35] The main eucharistic prayer in the first order for Holy Communion in the Church of Scotland's *Book of Common Order* contains the lines: "In this present time, we on earth have communion with you in heaven. But in the time to come, we shall be raised to that endless joy, prepared for us before the foundation of the world was laid." A further prayer gives assurance that "we belong to the company of all [Christ's] faithful people in heaven and on earth" and "will come to the glory of your eternal kingdom".[36] The second eucharistic prayer in the Scottish Episcopal Church's 1982 Liturgy states that Christ "opened the gate of glory and calls us now to share the life of heaven".[37] There are mentions of heavenly choirs in both communion and funeral liturgies. The latter tend to talk of "the sure and certain hope of resurrection" rather than specifically mention heaven, although among the scripture verses included for reading at the start of the Roman Catholic rite of committal is Philippians 3:20: "Our true home is in heaven, and Jesus Christ whose return we long for will come from heaven to save us."[38]

There are just a trickle of modern hymns and worship songs about heaven, compared with the torrent in the Victorian era surveyed in Chapter 1. One of the very few which seeks to describe and celebrate the post-mortem state, and does so with that image of heaven as home so prevalent in Victorian hymns, is "Going home, moving on, through God's open door" written in 1999 by the United Reformed Church minister, Michael Forster, to the tune from the slow movement from Dvorak's *New World Symphony* and found in both the Methodist hymn book *Singing the Faith* and the Anglican *Hymns Old and New*. John Bell, the Church of Scotland minister and member of the Iona Community's Wild Goose Worship Group, is another of the few who has written on this theme. His "The Last Journey", written in 1996, which begins "From the falter of breath, through the silence of death", explicitly mentions angels and heaven and echoes George Matheson in emphasizing that Christ has gone before us to welcome us there.[39] Along with Matheson's "O love that wilt not let me go" and Ellerton's "God of the living", it is on the list of hymns for my funeral.

For the most part, the contemporary Church keeps pretty stumm about heaven, and the afterlife barely features in sermons or even at funerals, which have now largely become memorial services focusing on life rather than on death and what may lie beyond it. There are undoubtedly challenges in highlighting heaven in the context of contemporary Christian practice and ministry. As Jacob Belder, vicar of the Pocklington group of churches in East Yorkshire, reflected in an article in the *Church Times* in 2021:

> As death becomes further removed from our purview by advances in health and medical technology, funerals become more a sort of memorial than anything else. Families wish to celebrate the life of the deceased rather than confront the reality of death. These expectations, combined with changes in modern funeral rites, make it easy, as N. T. Wright suggests in *Surprised by Hope* (2008) to do 'little to enlighten [mourners] and plenty to mislead them or confirm them in their existing muddle' about the afterlife.

Belder goes on to note how cremation, which now accounts for 81 per cent of all funerals in the UK (as against just 0.07 per cent in 1900), makes it even more difficult to focus on the afterlife. Rather than committing a body to the hallowed ground of a churchyard, next to "a building that has stood for hundreds and hundreds of years as a testament to the resurrection":

> you find yourself in a sterilised Chapel, merely a function room that is often far removed from the community in which the deceased lived, and in which the final moments of the body's passage to its final resting place are almost entirely mechanized...
>
> In a place that simply seems to absorb the body into a void, a signal of a return to nothingness, profoundly disjoined from the hope of resurrection, we are called to speak. Telling, in this regard, is the fact that funeral directors have whole shelves in their storerooms filled with ashes that family members never come to collect.[40]

The ubiquity of cremation does certainly make it more difficult for us now to relate to those poems by Christina Rossetti about graveyard flowers and to that extensive Victorian literature on life coming out of death inspired by observation of the circle of life, and the cycle of decay and rebirth in nature. Perhaps the welcome trend towards more eco-friendly and "green" funerals and natural woodland burials will bring us closer to this aspect of Victorian thinking and make the writings of Rossetti, F. W. Robertson and others quoted in Chapter 9 more relevant again.

As the opening up to death that seems to be happening in our own times continues, there will surely be more thought given to what may come after it and more echoing of those questions about heaven which so preoccupied the Victorians. Unless they want to continue to leave the field open to clairvoyants, mediums, tarot card readers, crystal gazers and other purveyors of esoteric religion, the churches, and Christians generally, will need to engage more with the subject of heaven and with the questions about it that many people have.

What distinguishes those whose extensive and considered meditations and reflections on heaven have filled this book above all is their deep pastoral instincts and their rich imaginations. I believe that both pastorally and imaginatively, they can help us address the questions of those who are close to death or fearful about it and wondering what may lie beyond it. They can also more directly help us ourselves as we contemplate that unknown country to which we are all journeying.

Ultimately, our own thoughts on heaven can only be guided by faith and hope, supplemented by imagination, intuition, reflection and reason and drawing on the somewhat scanty hints about it that are given in the Bible. The Victorians have been there before us and have thought about it more extensively, deeply and imaginatively than we do today. As such, they can be our guides. Some will find consolation in their hymns about homecoming and reuniting with family and friends. Others may be able to do no more than stretch forth the lame hand of faith with Alfred Tennyson and faintly trust the larger hope. Those drawn to angels may find much in the poems of Adelaide Procter and John Henry Newman that speaks directly to them. John Ellerton's sense of the dead living on unto and with God chimes with the process theology of Charles Hartshorne and others and with the thoughts of John Polkinghorne and

Paul Badham about the ways that we might be held in the divine memory. The emphasis put by F. D. Maurice, Benjamin Jowett and others on the activity to be found in heaven and its progressive nature will appeal to those who, like me at the age of 16, are not enamoured of an eternal existence sitting on a cloud, strumming a harp. I myself will, as I have done for 50 years or more, take strength, comfort and inspiration from George Matheson's vision of a return to the ocean depths of God's love from whence we came and will share it with those who ask me what heaven is going to be like:

> O Love that will not let me go,
> I rest my weary soul in thee.
> I give thee back the life I owe,
> that in thine ocean depths its flow
> may richer, fuller be.

## Notes

[1] Philippe Ariès, *Western Attitudes Toward Death* (Baltimore: Johns Hopkins University Press, 1974), p. 88.

[2] Yuval Noah Harari, "Will coronavirus change our attitudes to death?", *The Guardian*, 20 April 2020.

[3] Pat Jalland, *Death in the Victorian Family* (Oxford: Oxford University Press, 1996), pp. 57–8.

[4] Sogyal Rinpoche, *The Tibetan Book of Living and Dying* (London: Ebury Publishing, 1995), p. 7.

[5] William James, *Varieties of Religious Experience* (London: Longmans Green, 1903), p. 524.

[6] James Frazer, *The Belief in Immortality*, Vol. 1 (London: Macmillan, 1913), p. 33.

[7] George Orwell, *Seeing Things as They Are: Selected Journalism and Other Writings* (London: Penguin, 2016), p. 13.

8   D. MacEwan, *Missing Persons: Individual Eschatology in Twentieth Century Protestant Eschatology* (doctoral thesis, Trinity College, Dublin, 2000), pp. 5, 136.
9   MacEwan, *Missing Persons*, p. 226.
10  MacEwan, *Missing Persons*, p. 275.
11  N. T. Wright, *The Resurrection of the Son of God* (London: SPCK, 2003), p. 682.
12  Paul Badham, *Christian Beliefs about Life after Death* (London: SPCK, 1978), p. 146.
13  Paul Badham, *Immortality or Extinction?* (London: SPCK, 1984), p. 122.
14  Paul Badham, *Making Sense of Death and Immortality* (London: SPCK, 2013), p. 31.
15  John Hick, *Death and Eternal Life* (London: Collins, 1976), pp. 456, 463.
16  Karl Rahner, *On the Theology of Death*, in A. R. Caponigri, *Modern Catholic Thinkers: An Anthology* (London: Burns & Oates, 1961), p. 17.
17  Rahner, *On the Theology of Death*, p. 20.
18  Hans Küng, *Eternal Life?*, trans. E. Quinn (London: Collins, 1984), pp. 180–2.
19  C. McDannell and Bernhard Lang, *Heaven: A History* (New York: Vintage Books, 1990), p. 352.
20  Bernhard Lang, "Heaven", in *The Oxford Companion to Christian Thought* (Oxford: Oxford University Press, 2000), p. 388.
21  Brian Hebblethwaite, "Immortality", in *The Oxford Companion to Christian Thought* (Oxford: Oxford University Press, 2000), p. 321.
22  Lucy Bregman, "Death and Dying", in *The Cambridge Dictionary of Christian Theology* (Cambridge: Cambridge University Press, 2011), p. 131.
23  Sue Black, *All That Remains: A Life in Death* (London: Doubleday, 2018).
24  Government figures quoted in A. Bone, "What is the impact of population ageing on the future provision of end-of-life care?", *Palliative Medicine* 32:2 (2018).
25  Harari, "Will coronavirus change our attitudes to death?".
26  *The Value of Death*, Report of Lancet Commission, 31 January 2022, p. 1.
27  *The Value of Death*, p. 5.
28  *The Value of Death*, p. 12.
29  <https://yougov.co.uk/topics/society/articles-reports/2021/10/06/yougov-death-study-britons-life-after-death>, accessed 10 March 2023.

30. Marion Chatterley, *The Art of Dying Well*, Grosvenor Essay No. 9 (Edinburgh: The Scottish Episcopal Church, 2013), pp. 54, 56.
31. Peter Stanford, *Heaven: A Traveller's Guide to an Undiscovered Country* (London: HarperCollins, 2002), p. 356.
32. <https://www.artofdyingwell.org/what-is-dying-well/spiritual-questions/big-questions-death/>, accessed 10 March 2023.
33. Richard Holloway, *Waiting for the Last Bus* (Edinburgh: Canongate, 2018), p. 84.
34. Martin Camroux, email sent to author, 28 April 2018.
35. *Common Worship* (London: Church House Publishing, 2000), pp. 195, 197.
36. *Book of Common Order* (Edinburgh: St Andrew Press, 1994), pp. 133, 141.
37. Chatterley, *The Art of Dying Well*, p. 60.
38. *Order for Christian Funerals* (London: Geoffrey Chapman, 1990), p. 23.
39. John Bell, *The Last Journey* (Glasgow: Wild Goose Resource Group, 1996), p. 22. This hymn is quoted in full in my book *The Quiet Haven: An Anthology of Readings on Death and Heaven* (London: Darton, Longman & Todd, 2021), pp. 165–6.
40. Jacob Belder, "The Body of Our Low Estate", *Church Times*, 29 October 2021.

EU GPSR Authorized Representative:

LOGOS EUROPE, 9 rue Nicolas Poussin, 17000 La Rochelle, France

contact@logoseurope.eu